Jesus in the Everyday

A TWENTY-EIGHT WEEK DEVOTIONAL

Mitzi Ivey

Mitzi Ivey
www.findingthemore.org

Book Layout ©2017 BookDesignTemplates.com

Ordering Information:

Jesus in the Everyday/ Mitzi Ivey. —1st ed.

ISBN 978-1-7349162-1-8 (Paperback)

ISBN 978-1-7349162-0-1 (Ebook)

Contents

To my Saviour, the One who gave purpose to all my broken pieces
and
To my husband, who loves and supports me in all my madness!

WAYS TO USE THIS DEVOTIONAL

After working in ministry for several years, I have come to realize everyone doesn't do well with a lengthy study. Some prefer studies that have an element for each day and some women prefer to only be in a study one, maybe two days a week. This devotional is designed to fit the needs of many individuals. The basic layout is to read one devotion each week. Following each devotion is a weekly reflection section that poses four thoughts, questions, or scriptures to focus on.

If you prefer small doses for each day, then read the devotion one day and then do a section of the weekly reflection for the next four days. This method allows for quiet time five days each week.

If your method of quiet time is to set aside one day a week for more time, you could do the devotional and the weekly reflection all at one sitting.

To get the most out of each devotion it would be better to read and reflect on what you have read one day and then pick at least one other day to go through the weekly reflection thoughts but work within the time you have.

However, you choose to go through this devotional, I pray that you will invite the Holy Spirit to join you each time before you start. May the Holy Spirit fill you to overflow that you will be able to pour into others.

LET'S GET STARTED
Bible
Notebook
Pen

Introduction

A few years ago, I was working with a young girl in her 20's. One day she asked me how long before I finished the book I was always reading. I explained that I was reading through the Bible and try to do it at least once a year. Looking at me puzzled she asked, "If you have read the Bible, why do you need to read it again?" I tried telling her that the Bible is a living word which means it can speak to us in new ways every time we read it and that God uses His word to help us through what we are facing but the more I explained and the more scripture I brought out, the more confused she got. This heartbreaking encounter left me defeated, but also challenged me on how I was going to share Jesus with not only her but others in the same predicament.

After much prayer and many blessings from the Holy Spirit, God put it on my heart to look for Jesus in the everyday. So, I started looking for things people can relate to and understand. When we take what we come in contact with on a daily basis and find scripture or a biblical principle, then we can help others see Jesus in what they know, and the connection starts to build a foundation to grow on.

A lack of biblical knowledge can create a challenge when trying to share the gospel, but it wasn't always this way. There was a time when people had some type of exposure to scripture. Even if you didn't grow up in church, there was more than likely a vacation bible school in the neighborhood or a friend that went to Sunday school and shared what they learned. Such as a bunch of animals getting on a giant boat two by two. Even high school literature books had books of the bible! Although they weren't acknowledged as the bible, we still studied them as being great literature. Times have changed and the exposure is gone which has left a whole generation that has never heard of the ark, the parting of the red sea, Moses and the ten commandments, the cross, the resurrection...the bible is foreign to them and without any knowledge, our attempts to share our faith through scriptures can become overwhelming for them and challenging for us. Nevertheless, we must find a way to reach them.

I've found that seeing Jesus in the ordinary things of life makes it so much more extraordinary to share the hope that lives within us through Christ. God gives us daily reminders that He is not only to be found at church, but everywhere, all the time, which helps us remember that He is in every aspect of our lives. Once we realize this, then it will help us find more in our walk with Jesus. It doesn't take great theology to tell someone about the amazing God we serve, just a love for our Saviour.

This devotional is meant to open your heart to see scripture and biblical principles in a remarkable way. My hope is that after reading this devotional you will see that Jesus is in the everyday aspects of our world and that learning to see Him in all things will renew your hope and allow you to encourage others.

✳

Labels

When we go to an event or conference, one of the first things they have you do is put on a name tag. Sometimes it simply has your name, or it might list your church, business or maybe your hometown. These types of labels are used to identify us and make it easier for other people to know who we are.

There are labels that we wear which might not look like a name tag for all see, but they are labels none the less. Some labels are good and help us to stand confident in who God designed us to be, but there are also labels that can make us feel less than. We go through experiences in our life that can leave an impact that may affect us to the very core, but our experiences don't have to define us.

In scripture we read about Rahab in the book of Joshua chapter two. Now Rahab is listed as a harlot, that is her label which, in biblical times, was even more vulgar than it is in today's world. Rahab is even listed in Hebrews chapter eleven in what people refer to as the Hall of Faith. Yet, interestingly enough, she is still referred to as the harlot. Now Rahab is so much more than a harlot! I could think of several labels to give her such as resourceful, loyal, faithful... Rahab is also David's great grandmother, which places her in the lineage of Jesus. You see, Rahab could have stayed just the harlot and not risked her life to save the spies from Israel, but she did risk her life because she believed in this big God that the spies served. She did not allow the label of who she was to determine who God had created her to be.

We also learn of Hannah over in 1 Samuel chapter one who was barren. She was made fun of for her inability to have a child, but rather than accept that label, she poured her heart out to God and she was no longer sad (verse18). Hannah trusted that God would be faithful. It says in verse 19 that she worshipped God before He even answered her prayers. God later honored her prayers with not only one child, but she was blessed with five children in all. Now, Hannah could have taken the label of barren and never put it into God's hands. She could have lived out her days accepting a label that was given her but instead she refused to let it stick and chose to trust God.

One of my favorite things about labels, they are not permanent. Like a sticky note, we choose what sticks and what falls off. Only we can sift through and determine if we will accept a label and even then, we get to choose if it defines us or not.

Negative Labels

We all have been called a name or two in our lives. Some labels (names) are easy to hear and some- not so much. We usually aren't affected by the nicer labels we receive such as being pretty, smart, polite, nice, or kind. These types of labels rarely stick and while they may make us smile for a moment, we rarely take them in and let them define us. Don't get me wrong, a nice label is an encouragement, and we generally are happy to hear nice things, but overall, most people don't spend much time on them.

For some sad reason, we are however, more prone to allow the negative labels spoken or sometimes even written about us to stick. We take all the negative labels to heart. These labels can settle down deep and begin to define who we are. Now we shouldn't be surprised when the world tags us with negative labels, because even Jesus was tagged with a few… gluttonous, winebibber, a lawbreaker, friend to sinners, and they said He was of Beelzebub when He cast out demons. Worse part, Jesus was given these labels by the Pharisees (religious leaders).

Jesus lived a perfect and sinless life in a corrupt world, yet He was still assigned negative labels, all of which were not true. If the only perfect person to walk this earth was labeled negatively by this world, we can't expect our fallible lives to go unscathed. The struggle comes when we allow those labels to stick and define who we are. Old Lucifer would like nothing better than for us to crawl through life allowing these negative labels to keep us defeated. So, rather than walk as a child of the King, we begin to crawl through life believing the negative labels that we are worthless or   less   than.

This world will label you:

Nothing	Unlovable	Stupid
Trash	A Mistake	Damaged
Useless	Worthless	Broken
Loser	Disgusting	Invisible

You may have been told you will never amount to anything, and that you have never been anything except pointless, but that is NOT your truth.

If we allow these negative labels to define us, we will become bitter, harbor hatred, and stay buried in the dark. Let me remind you that Jesus came to dispel the darkness and by His glorious light, the darkness must flee. We cannot let others define who we are! Only God created us and only He determines who we are.

So, stop allowing the words of others to label you.

BUT WHEN THE PHARISEES HEARD [IT], THEY SAID, THIS [FELLOW] DOTH NOT CAST OUT DEVILS, BUT BY BEELZEBUB THE PRINCE OF THE DEVILS. MATTHEW 12:24
THE SON OF MAN COMES EATING AND DRINKING; AND YE SAY, BEHOLD A GLUTTONOUS MAN, AND A WINEBIBBER, A FRIEND OF PUBLICANS AND SINNERS! LUKE 7:34
How does it make you feel to know that even Jesus had to endure negativity?

Are there any negative labels that you have allowed others to assign to you? We cannot stop others from being negative, but we can choose to not let them stick. Write out any negative labels you may have allowed the world to tag you with and then give each one to Jesus, refusing to wear them any longer.

THEN SPAKE JESUS AGAIN UNTO THEM, SAYING, I AM THE LIGHT OF THE WORLD: HE THAT FOLLOWETH ME SHALL NOT WALK IN DARKNESS, BUT SHALL HAVE THE LIGHT OF LIFE. JOHN 8:12
Are you allowing the darkness of this world to extinguish the light within you? Christ said that we would not walk in darkness, so do not let the negative labels of this world put you in darkness. Ask the Lord to

illuminate any part of your life that may be covered in darkness.

WHO HATH DELIVERED US FROM THE POWER OF DARKNESS AND HATH TRANSLATED [US] INTO THE KINGDOM OF HIS DEAR SON: COLOSSIANS 1:13

Take time to remind yourself that you are delivered. Put on your new name, Child of the King!

Self-Label

I want to start by saying that I don't know of one single person that does not carry a self-label. Now this is a label you have assigned yourself it might be true of who you were, but if you are a child of God, it will not be true of who you are today.

We all have things from our past that we could be labeled for. For some of us that could have been years ago and for others it could have been just a few minutes ago. Regardless of elapsed time, our mistakes or sins do not have to become the name we answer to, it does not have to define us.

Most of us have made mistakes that have altered our lives, and sometimes the lives of others, but that mistake does not have to become what we answer to for the rest of our lives. We can be much harder on ourselves than others in some circumstances. Bad choices, moments of anger and downright poor actions can take on a life of their own, and rather than acknowledge them, repent, and move forward we allow them to hold us hostage.

We label ourselves - not enough, loser, barren, failure, harlot, liar, abused, mistake, victim and the list could go on and on. On paper these are simple words but when we believe they represent who we have become, then they have great power. I want to say something right here and I hope you hear these words...

If you have been abused, whether physical, mental or both in any fashion, you are not defined by what has happened to you. You are not a victim; you are an amazing and beautiful person that may have been a victim of trauma but that is not who you are and no one, not even yourself should allow these labels to define you.

While I'm on my box... we, in ourselves, can never be enough because if we could, then we would never need a Saviour. Yes, I am not enough by myself, nor will I ever be, and it is perfectly okay because I serve a living God that is more than enough for me and He is more than enough for you, too!

The sad part is that most of us have allowed these self-labels to keep us in bondage long after it was covered by the blood. When we surrender our lives to Jesus, asking for forgiveness and turning from our sins, He cleanses us and makes us a new creature. Yes, we will still sin, but God is gracious and will forgive us our sins if we will ask. So, if you have asked the Lord to forgive you why are you still wearing the label.

I struggled with God's forgiveness because in honesty... I know that I don't deserve it. I would say, "I know that God has forgiven me and saved me, but I am worthless and should not be forgiven, so I disqualify myself from being able to serve." The problem with this thought is I was unknowingly putting myself greater than God. You see, when we think this way and wear our labels of the old self, we are truly saying that God's word is not true and that He cannot do what He has said.

Now we don't think that is what we are saying, but it is what we are living. God's word is true and when God said He would make us a new creature, then we are new. When God said He would cleanse us from all unrighteousness and make us the children of God, we must stand in that truth which is impossible to do if we are wearing old labels.

TO ALLOW CHRIST TO CHANGE YOU, YOU MUST FIRST LET GO OF WHO YOU THINK YOU ARE!

Weekly Reflection

Are there things from your past that you are allowing to define or limit who Christ would have you to be? Take some time with the Lord and write out what He puts in your heart.

THEREFORE, IF ANY MAN BE IN CHRIST, HE IS A NEW CREATURE: OLD THINGS ARE PASSED AWAY; BEHOLD, ALL THINGS ARE BECOME NEW. 2 CORINTHIANS 5:17
Last time I checked, all meant all. Write out the things Christ has made new in your life and spend time rejoicing that the old is passed away.

IF WE CONFESS OUR SINS, HE IS FAITHFUL AND JUST TO FORGIVE US OUR SINS, AND TO CLEANSE US FROM ALL UNRIGHTEOUSNESS. 1 JOHN 1:9
Is there something you have not asked God to forgive you for, is there something you have done that you are refusing to forgive yourself for? Write it out and surrendering it all to Him, trusting that He is able to cleanse you fully.

Write out Galatians 2:20 and remember that you are now living by the power of Christ in you, and you don't have the right to label yourself anything other than His.

Idealized Labels

One type of label we often wear is the idealized label. The idealized label is the label that many of us wear to appease others. We don't trust others to know who we are, or we are afraid that if others knew the real us, they would leave; therefore, we wear the idealized label to hide who we are.

There is a real problem in our society today, especially with social media that says we all need to have some form of fabulousness. We need the house, the cars, the jobs, the kids, and all of it well kept and in order. So, we go around trying to live up to a particular standard that is impossible to maintain 24/7.

In reality, most of the things people post on social media are less than 1% of their daily lives. Some people spend more time putting it all together to get one quick pic than they actually spend living in the day to day. We all have dreams, and we might even be living in the middle of that perfect life right now but most of us are not.

Even when we know that most of the pictures are fake and that the struggle is real, we somehow can still fall into the trap of living an idealized labeled life. We put on the happy face and tell everyone we are fine, life is good, our marriage is good, our kids are great, and we couldn't ask for anything else; when in reality we know that behind that smile, the struggle is real and we don't even feel like getting out of bed.

We are taught not to say marriage is hard, my kids have lost their minds and if one more thing breaks at the house I might just scream because in all honesty, who wants to hear the truth. So, we just say fine or great, put on the idealized label, smile, and push on through while we scream on the inside wishing just one person really knew us.

As a human being we all long, at some level, to be known. Not to just be superficially known by our name tag but for someone to really know us and not label us or turn us away. The thought of someone rejecting us if we let them in is so terrifying that we find it easier to just pretend. So, we walk around showing our idealized label and hide the person we are.

One of the greatest truths I have ever come to realize is that there is one person that knows me fully and for some reason beyond me, He still loves me completely. God knows everything about all of us. He knows the good, the bad, the ugly and even the most shameful things we have ever done in this life or will ever do and surprisingly enough, He also loves us more than anyone else in the universe. Jesus took on the pain and heartache of all my sins and yours, so we could one day live with Him for eternity, even before we were willing to live for Him. Christ died so we can live, not as someone we are not, but as a child of the King.

I'm going to share this with you again in this series, because repetition never hurts. God did not design you to live in shame. He sacrificed His only Son (Jesus Christ) that you could be free from the bondage of your sins and made new. If you are a child of the King, your past is covered by the blood. Don't let what God has forgotten have power over you. Only God's labels are true.

Weekly Reflection

Are you wearing any idealized labels when you are around others? Are you even wearing them when you are at home trying to be who you think others want you to be? Ask God to help you be who He designed you to be.

WHOSE ADORNING LET IT NOT BE THAT OUTWARD [ADORNING] OF PLAITING THE HAIR, AND OF WEARING OF GOLD, OR OF PUTTING ON OF APPAREL; BUT [LET IT BE] THE HIDDEN MAN OF THE HEART, IN THAT WHICH IS NOT CORRUPTIBLE, [EVEN THE ORNAMENT] OF A MEEK AND QUIET SPIRIT, WHICH IS IN THE SIGHT OF GOD OF GREAT PRICE. 1 PETER 3:3-4

The most important part about us is our hearts. We can fix up our outer person (wear that idealized label) but if we haven't cleaned up our hearts, it is all in vain. Is there some area that you still try to hide? If so, give it to God and let Him minister to your heart.

FAVOUR [IS] DECEITFUL, AND BEAUTY [IS] VAIN: [BUT] A WOMAN [THAT] FEARETH THE LORD, SHE SHALL BE PRAISED. PROVERBS 31:30

There is nothing wrong with dressing up or wanting to look nice but if it is only for us to get approval from others so they will think more highly of us, then we are wearing an idealized label trying to measure up. If you have a heart for the Lord, then you don't need to be anything but who He designed you to be. Be still and let the Lord reveal if there is anyone you are trying to impress.

You get to decide the you; you present to the world! Take a moment and write out who you are and what you   want   others   to   see   in   you.

God's Label

I'm so excited to share this label with you and it has taken all that I have to not spoil it by falling off track in the other devotions. This week we are going to talk about the only label that matters... God's label.

You see, from the very beginning of time God knew you, yes you. He knew exactly who you were going to be and all the mistakes you were going to make. God designed you specifically in all your unique and wonderful ways. The Lord put a burning desire in your soul to need Him and to worship Him for all your days, now and for eternity.

We may have been many things before we gave our lives to Christ. We may have answered to "less than" labels before we came to know the Saviour, but when we put our trust in Jesus, God cleanses us of all our sins. We then become who He designed us to be. No longer are we a slave in bondage to sin, but now we are free in Christ, a new creature.

Believing who God made you to be and allowing all the wonderful labels He has for you is not easy to accept, especially if you have had a sinful past. The darkness of your past can be difficult to move beyond, but if you will spend time in the Word, learning more about who God is, then you will learn to trust Him more fully. Then when you trust God completely in who He is, you can begin to accept who He says you are.

Until you believe God fully, you will want to hold tight to your old labels because even in pain there is comfort in the known. Yet, with God's grace, you will find real comfort by drawing closer to Him.

I know it is mind blowing to think that the very God that created the universe - the stars, the mountains, the oceans, and all the wonders of the world, would take the time to thoughtfully, uniquely create you but it is true. Not only does He take the time to know each of us, but He loves us, truly loves us more than anything you or me could ever comprehend, I promise!

You see once we can embrace the truth of God's love and learn to live in that love believing who He says we are, then we can put all of God's labels on our lives. His truth will drastically alter how we live because we will finally know that it is no longer about us. We will trust that He is our Father, and it is He who has us.

Here are just a few of the labels God has for His children:

Chosen	Blessed	Forgiven
Treasured	Soldier	Masterpiece
Special	Unique	Divine Purpose
Beautiful	Loveable	Apple of His Eye

And my favorite is child of the King which makes me smile because anyway you say it, I am HIS!

Today, start relabeling yourself with God's truth!

Weekly Reflection

I WILL PRAISE THEE; FOR I AM FEARFULLY [AND] WONDERFULLY MADE: MARVELLOUS [ARE] THY WORKS; AND [THAT] MY SOUL KNOWETH RIGHT WELL. PSALM 139:14

ACCORDING AS HE HATH CHOSEN US IN HIM BEFORE THE FOUNDATION OF THE WORLD, THAT WE SHOULD BE HOLY AND WITHOUT BLAME BEFORE HIM IN LOVE: HAVING PREDESTINATED US UNTO THE ADOPTION OF CHILDREN BY JESUS CHRIST TO HIMSELF, ACCORDING TO THE GOOD PLEASURE OF HIS WILL, TO THE PRAISE OF THE GLORY OF HIS GRACE, WHEREIN HE HATH MADE US ACCEPTED IN THE BELOVED. EPHESIANS 1:4-6

Read these verses a few times and let them sink in that you are one of His masterpieces. Because of the blood of Christ, we can be blameless before Him knowing that Christ has made us accepted. Write down the parts that stand out to you the most in these verses and let God speak to you through them.

Of the labels listed in the devotion, which one is the hardest for you to believe about yourself? Which one means the most to your heart? Write out your response below.

Look up Romans 8:14-17. Write out what it means to be a child of God, to know that we can cry out to Him as Father.

STAND FAST THEREFORE IN THE LIBERTY WHEREWITH CHRIST HATH MADE US FREE AND BE NOT ENTANGLED AGAIN WITH THE YOKE OF BONDAGE. GALATIANS 5:1
Is there an old label that you need to let go of, to stop being entangled to the bondage that Christ has freed you from? Surrender them all to God and if you have already been able to do this, then take time to praise Him for your freedom.

Cupcakes

What kind of cupcake are you? And even more importantly, what kind of cupcake would you like to be? I'm sure you are thinking, "Cupcake, what are you talking about?" Over the next five weeks, we will be looking at the different types of cupcakes and learning how they can relate to our Christian walk.

If you have ever baked cupcakes, you know that it doesn't take much to ruin the whole batch. If you mix the batter too long, they can become hard. One too many eggs or not enough and the texture will be off. Forget to look at the recipe and set the oven too high, the cupcakes will burn, and if the temperature is too low, they will take forever to bake.

Our Christian walk can be the same way! We need to spend time in the Word every day allowing God to soften our hearts, so we won't become hard. God has supplied us with the perfect recipe that comes out superbly every time, but are we taking the time to look at the recipe? When we follow God's recipe, He will lead us in our day-to-day lives and make us into the cupcake   He   wants   us   to   be.

The Mega Cupcake

I really enjoy going to a good bakery and seeing all the specialty items, especially the large decadent cupcakes. You know, the really big ones that are a little too much cupcake for one person but truly not enough to share. (Well, not at my house anyway!) They usually come in outrageous flavors like Cherry Lemon Sundrop, Death by Chocolate, Sea Salt Caramel... which makes it difficult to pick just one. As you stare into the case, you think, "I really don't need that big of a cupcake but at the same time, your belly is explaining to your head that just one won't be too bad."

Might I share with you that some Christians are like the mega cupcake, they can be very excited, but a bit too much, all at the same time. I generally refer to these type of followers as "Puffed Up". My grandmother would have said, "they just a little too big for their britches!"

The mega cupcake Christian enjoys showing off their scriptural knowledge to everyone they encounter, whether asked to or not. They have such a plethora of knowledge, or at least they believe they do, that they can't help but talk about it all the time. (their knowledge, not Jesus)

They have a verse for every occasion whether it applies to the situation or not. If you accidently misspeak or reference something wrong, don't worry, the mega cupcake will be all too ready to correct you openly so all will know that they have the answer. They also enjoy sharing all the good they have done for the Lord. They drop in a side note in each conversation about the money they gave, the card they sent, or the food they donated, as they would not like for any good deed to go unnoticed.

Along our faith walk, we will inadvertently get a little prideful, especially if we're not continually surrendering our lives to Christ. Don't get me wrong, we should be bragging on all that God is doing, but we also need to be checking in to make sure it is about what God does and not what we are doing so we don't become puffed up.

If we over-inflate our abilities, or our wisdom, it can be a hard place to fall from. A good checkup is to ask ourselves each night, "Did I talk more about me and what I can do, or did I talk more about the Lord and all He is doing?"

Weekly Reflection

BRETHREN, IF A MAN BE OVERTAKEN IN A FAULT, YE WHICH ARE SPIRITUAL, RESTORE SUCH AN ONE IN THE SPIRIT OF MEEKNESS; CONSIDERING THYSELF, LEST THOU ALSO BE TEMPTED. GALATIANS 6:1

We need to be mindful that all of us can get a mega cupcake mentality. So, we should not look down on others behaving this way. Instead, we should pray for them and be alert, so we do not fall into this same mindset.

In the space below confess any area in your life that you may be looking down on others for being too much and then take a moment to lift-up them up to the Lord.

AND THESE THINGS, BRETHREN, I HAVE IN A FIGURE TRANSFERRED TO MYSELF AND [TO] APOLLOS FOR YOUR SAKES; THAT YE MIGHT LEARN IN US NOT TO THINK [OF MEN] ABOVE THAT WHICH IS WRITTEN, THAT NO ONE OF YOU BE PUFFED UP FOR ONE AGAINST ANOTHER. 1 CORINTHIANS 4:6

Take time to let the Lord show you any area in your life that you are living "puffed up" because of comparison.

Take a moment and write out 1 Corinthians 8:2, just let the Lord speak to you.

CHARITY SUFFERETH LONG, [AND] IS KIND; CHARITY ENVIETH NOT; CHARITY VAUNTETH NOT ITSELF, IS NOT PUFFED UP, *1 CORINTHIANS 13:4*

We are to love one another not by vain words or high-mindedness but with pure motives. We are to love our neighbors not because they deserve it but simply because God loves us and gave Himself for us. Who could you show love to today without a need for recognition?

Factory-Made Cupcake

In a rush, a good old individually wrapped, store-bought factory-made cupcake will fix a sugar craving. When it comes to this cupcake, you know what you are getting, a machined uniform treat. (I must admit, it makes me a little jealous, my cupcakes rarely taste the same, much less look the same.)

The problem with a factory-made cupcake is it has no character; each one is designed to be exactly like the next one. Now this uniformity is great for appearance, but it has no depth. God doesn't want us to be factory-made Christians. Scripture teaches us that God has designed each of us to be unique. We are not meant to be a knock-off version of some other child of God, but He has purposefully created each of us with a divine calling in the kingdom.

We are taught by the world that we need to try to look like other people, speak like other people, and try to be just like other people, but God explains in His Word that we are each unique in design and that He doesn't need us to be someone else but exactly who He created us to be. The Bible teaches us that blood bought children of God are all one body but many members. We are not supposed to fight over who gets to be the hands or who gets to be the feet, but we should be spending time with the Lord and let Him show us our place.

When we first get saved, we can fall into the trap of looking at other Christians and wanting what they have or striving to do what they do. Yes, we all need to learn by example and help each other but God did not call me to be you or you to be me. Even the most put together Christian has imperfections, flaws, and weakness but by God's grace and the blood of Jesus Christ we are justified to be able to bring Him glory by being who He designed us to be.

So, take some time this week to ask God to reveal to you where you may be trying to make yourself into someone else. Once you acknowledge where you are mimicking others, you will be able to clearly see and become the person you were meant to be.

Weekly Reflection

I WILL PRAISE THEE; FOR I AM FEARFULLY [AND] WONDERFULLY MADE: MARVELLOUS [ARE] THY WORKS; AND [THAT] MY SOUL KNOWETH RIGHT WELL. PSALM *139:14*

Why would you want to be someone else? God has made you unique for His glorious purpose. Take time to praise God for all the wonderful ways He created you to be uniquely you!

BUT YE [ARE] A CHOSEN GENERATION, A ROYAL PRIESTHOOD, AN HOLY NATION, A PECULIAR PEOPLE; THAT YE SHOULD SHEW FORTH THE PRAISES OF HIM WHO HATH CALLED YOU OUT OF DARKNESS INTO HIS MARVELLOUS LIGHT: 1 PETER *2:9*

Merriam-Webster Dictionary defines peculiar two ways:
1. characteristic of only one person, group, or thing: DISTINCTIVE
2. something exempt from ordinary jurisdiction

Strong's Defines Peculiar:
1. being beyond usual, i.e. special (one's own)

How does this definition change your outlook on the above verse?

Now that you know the definition of peculiar, read Titus 2:14. Does this verse have more meaning?

NOW THERE ARE DIVERSITIES OF GIFTS, BUT THE SAME SPIRIT. AND THERE ARE DIFFERENCES OF ADMINISTRATIONS, BUT THE SAME LORD. *1 CORINTHIANS 12:4-5*

Ask God to show you the unique talents He created you with and how He wants you to use them for His glory.

Beautiful Cupcake

Have you ever bought or been given a cupcake that is so beautifully made that you hate to bite into it? The kind of cupcake that has perfectly swirled icing with shaved chocolate pieces that twirl into gorgeous monuments that adorn the top making you wonder if it is fake.

Now, I have experienced this type of magnificent treat, and I discovered that how it looks and how it taste are rarely of the same grandeur. Yes, this beautiful cupcake can be very deceiving. The truth of the matter is sometimes things that look appealing can be too good to be true. I have had the unfortunate privilege to get very excited about a beautiful cupcake only to find out that it tastes like dirt on the inside. The beautiful cupcake Christian is characterized by looking great on the outside but being less than taste worthy on the inside.

A cupcake is meant to be eaten and enjoyed, but if it tastes terrible what is the point of having a cupcake. I'm sure you have come across this type of treat before. Jesus spoke often of the hypocrisy of the religious leaders of His time. He even told the people to follow them in word but not in deed, because they talked a good game and worked diligently to make sure everyone else was following the law but they themselves were wicked on the inside.

We live in a time where outward appearance is emphasized as a necessity, and the need for a clean heart is ignored. It is as if the culture is saying it is okay to be ugly and deceitful inside, as long as no one sees it. As children of God, we must remember that He does not look on our outer person, but He looks at our hearts. So, if our hearts are wicked, what value is our outer beauty? Just like the cupcake, if it just looks good but taste terrible, what is the value?

When we give our lives to God, He begins to change our lives from the inside out. He converts our minds and changes our hearts to be like Him. When our attitude changes and our focus is on Jesus, our outer person will be something beautiful because others will see the Jesus who dwells in our hearts, rather than us.

Would you rather people see your own beauty or His beauty shining through you?

Weekly Reflection

BUT THE LORD SAID UNTO SAMUEL, LOOK NOT ON HIS COUNTENANCE, OR ON THE HEIGHT OF HIS STATURE; BECAUSE I HAVE REFUSED HIM: FOR [THE LORD SEETH] NOT AS MAN SEETH; FOR MAN LOOKETH ON THE OUTWARD APPEARANCE, BUT THE LORD LOOKETH ON THE HEART. *1 SAMUEL 16:7*

Is there an area in your life that you have made look pretty on the outside so no one would know how ugly it is on the inside? If so, take a few moments to release that area to God and let Him begin to make the inside match the out.

FOR WHICH CAUSE WE FAINT NOT; BUT THOUGH OUR OUTWARD MAN PERISH, YET THE INWARD [MAN] IS RENEWED DAY BY DAY. *2 CORINTHIANS 4:16*

What are some ways you can make adjustments that will allow the Lord to renew your heart each day?

HAVING A FORM OF GODLINESS BUT DENYING THE POWER THEREOF: FROM SUCH TURN AWAY. *2 TIMOTHY 3:5*

Do you have a form of godliness that appears when you are at church or around certain people? Do you behave one way at the house of God and another at work or with your family? God, reveal any area where I only have a form of godliness.

AND THE LORD SAID UNTO HIM, NOW DO YE PHARISEES MAKE CLEAN THE OUTSIDE OF THE CUP AND THE PLATTER; BUT YOUR INWARD PART IS FULL OF RAVENING AND WICKEDNESS. LUKE 11:39
It doesn't matter how much time you spend being the perfect weight, applying the best beauty products, or wearing designer clothes if your heart is full of hate, judgement, pride.... Sometimes we don't even realize areas that we have allowed our hearts to become dirty. Ask Jesus to show you the places in your heart that need to be cleaned.

Mini Cupcakes

I enjoy a good cupcake and when I'm trying to eat healthier, a mini cupcake seems to be the ticket. A small treat to satisfy the sweet tooth! In our world today, most things come in a mini, but can I tell you when it comes to our Christian walk, mini is not the way to go.

Some people are mini cupcakes in their faith because they are new in Christ. They have surrendered their life, but all this faith walk stuff is new and let's be honest, new can be overwhelming and figuring it all out on our own is not easy. It is understandable that new believers have a lot to learn and will grow over time, but the difficulty comes when people simply decide they don't want to grow in the Lord, therefore, becoming content to stay "mini".

It doesn't take great theological knowledge or years of classes to grow. Small steps can have a big impact. One step in growing comes from spending time getting to know Who God is. This happens when we read our Bible and allow God's character to be revealed to us.

Next step is to spend time in conversation with God. When we pray to Him, it allows us to grow in fellowship with Him. This is also the perfect time to ask the Lord to reveal Himself to you through His Word.

Praise is huge for growing in Christ! If we learn to praise Him every day for all His blessings, it will become easier to trust Him regardless of our circumstances. In our praise we remind ourselves of God's faithfulness, goodness, and compassion which draws us to grow in our relationship with Him.

When we are new in Christ, we need to find a trusted mentor to lead us and guide us in our relationship, but the same is true for those of us who have been on this faith walk for many years.

We will never be able to reach all that God has purposed for us if we do not grow in our relationship with Christ. We must continually seek to know Him more and to grow in His word, but this can be difficult without the help of those who have already been there.

Lastly, mini cupcakes generally come in a multipack, and babes in Christ are no different. In general, babes do not like to be challenged or forced to grow, so they tend to hang out with people of like maturity. If everyone you spend time with is in the same place you are, then you will begin to think you must be fine. It goes back to the comparison theory which leads people to believe if the people they are around are okay then they must be okay too.

As children of God, we should always look for others who challenge us to grow in our relationship to the Lord. We should not stay where we are just because others are. Who knows, maybe if one of the cupcakes decided to grow, it might challenge the others to grow as well. We should never stay mini to accommodate those around us.

So, mini cupcakes need to focus on growing in Christ!

Weekly Reflections

AS NEWBORN BABES, DESIRE THE SINCERE MILK OF THE WORD, THAT YE MAY GROW THEREBY: 1 PETER 2:2 As children of God, we should have a desire to read the Word. Today, we have access to the Bible on our phones, tablets, and computers. Take some time to find a Bible Reading Plan that works with your schedule and prioritize time with God.

AND I, BRETHREN, COULD NOT SPEAK UNTO YOU AS UNTO SPIRITUAL, BUT AS UNTO CARNAL, EVEN AS UNTO BABES IN CHRIST. I HAVE FED YOU WITH MILK, AND NOT WITH MEAT: FOR HITHERTO YE WERE NOT ABLE TO BEAR IT, NEITHER YET NOW ARE YE ABLE. 1 CORINTHIANS 3:2 Do you enjoy hearing the beautiful accounts in the Bible of rescue and restoration but struggle to spend time asking for understanding on the hard things such as, we will face persecution. Take some time throughout your day to ask God if there are any areas of His word that you are avoiding because they seem too hard. Seek the wisdom of the Holy Spirit to help you begin to process those areas and seek a trusted mentor to grow with.

Schedule time this week to just sit with God so He can show you any areas in your life you need to be growing. As He guides, write them down so you can reflect on them and move towards a closer relationship with the Lord.

Do you have a trusted, faithful mentor, someone that can pray with you and go through the Bible? Do you have someone you can talk with that directs you back to God and His Word for help and encouragement? If the answer is yes, praise God for sending them into your life but if the answer is no, start praying about who God could use as a mentor in your life.

Smashed Cupcake

The smashed cupcake is that cupcake that doesn't always look that great but still tastes phenomenal. I have found that there are usually two distinct reasons why a cupcake doesn't look too great. Either it was handled a few too many times after being decorated, or it had a hard time coming out of the pan. On more than one occasion, I have worked extremely hard to decorate a cupcake spending way too much time making it pretty and not enough time planning transportation of the cupcake. When a cupcake is not secured properly, it can come out looking a little rough around the edges.

Some Christians have been through many adventures throughout their walk of faith and the bumps and bruises have left them a little ragged. They feel they have done their part, and it is now time for them to sit out for the remainder of their journey.

In theory, this is a much-appreciated concept but nowhere in the scriptures have I found a retirement plan that is available before heaven. When we are further on our journey, our ability to serve might look a little different from when we first started out, but that doesn't change the call to bring God glory.

Our cupcake might appear a little tattered from the journey, but it is still edible. One of the most encouraging parts of my faith walk is knowing that some of our more seasoned women are lifting me up to the Lord and being mighty prayer warriors for God's kingdom. Some of our seasoned saints have the gift of encouragement; they send out cards, call and pray for our congregation. Others have discovered that they have a lot to offer the mini cupcakes and spend time mentoring them along the way.

Now the second kind of smashed cupcake, the one that just gets stuck in the pan, I can truly relate with. I wasn't raised in church and lived a life that was way less than pleasing to God. I was saved in my mid-twenties and didn't come out of the pan all neat and pretty. I had many scares and was extremely damaged inside and out when the Lord delivered me. I have never looked like much to this world or to those closest to me, but I can now say, after a long journey, I have a lot to offer because of all Christ has done to change my heart.

We don't all wear our scars on the outside. Some of us have scars that run deep which might have made our lives fall apart a time or two, but God doesn't look at that. Our God picks up all our crumbs (brokenness), pipes some icing with a few sprinkles (grace & mercy) on top and calls us a cupcake (His child).

Some of the best cupcakes I've ever eaten didn't look like much but tasted amazing and I usually enjoyed them standing in my kitchen, surrounded by a mess, thanking God for all He had blessed me with.

Weekly Reflection

And she [was] a widow of about fourscore and four years, which departed not from the temple, but served [God] with fastings and prayers night and day. Luke 2:37

Have you believed the lie that you have served enough or that you are no longer useful for the kingdom because you can't do all the things you did before? The widow in the verse above dedicated herself to prayer and fasting. We can all pray, speak/write a word of encouragement, or simply check-in on a fellow sister regardless of our physical conditions. Write out some ways you can serve others.

BEHOLD, THOU DESIREST TRUTH IN THE INWARD PARTS: AND IN THE HIDDEN [PART] THOU SHALT MAKE ME TO KNOW WISDOM. PSALM 51:6

What lies have you been believing? You are a mess, not well versed, your past is too bad, you've broken too many commandments, you don't deserve to have a place.... All lies, lies that are meant to keep you from serving out your purpose. Stop holding onto those lies, write them below and let God have them. Then take time to let God tell you who He says you are and the calling He has for your life.

BUT JESUS TURNED HIM ABOUT, AND WHEN HE SAW HER, HE SAID, DAUGHTER, BE OF GOOD COMFORT; THY FAITH HATH MADE THEE WHOLE. AND THE WOMAN WAS MADE WHOLE FROM THAT HOUR. MATTHEW 9:22

The world would have called this woman damaged, broken, or worthless but Jesus lovingly looked at her and called her daughter. If you have accepted Jesus as Lord of your life, He calls you son/daughter now too! Write out how that speaks to your heart.

AND THE VESSEL THAT HE MADE OF CLAY WAS MARRED IN THE HAND OF THE POTTER: SO HE MADE IT AGAIN ANOTHER VESSEL, AS SEEMED GOOD TO THE POTTER TO MAKE [IT]. JEREMIAH 18:4

God knows all the ways in which we have been scarred by our lives. Some scars come from circumstances out of our control and others by poor choices, but the Lord can make all of it into something beautiful when we give it to Him. He isn't waiting on us to clean up before we come. God just wants us to come and give it all to Him and let Him make us new. What are you choosing not to reach for because of your scars?

Popcorn

It's nice to sit on the couch, curl up in a blanket and watch a movie. What makes that evening better? A bowl of warm buttery popcorn.

Today, we have the convenience of microwave popcorn that can be ready in two minutes flat. Quick, easy and if you don't smother it in butter or salt, a pretty healthy snack.

When you look in the bag you will notice that not all of the kernels are the same, yet in theory, each piece should come out identical. All are dried kernels of corn, all in the same bag, and all have been exposed to the same cooking process, and still, when poured out, you will see that some never popped, some partially popped, some are fully popped and on occasion they may even be burnt.

If you look at any group of people, you can find the same variety! Some people live behind a hard shell (kernels). Some give a little (half-popped). Others are all in (fully popped) and there are those who are burnt.

The next few weeks we will look at each type and how we may fall into the different categories. Now, the best part for us is we can determine which kernel we want to be. We are not stuck with what comes out the bag.

Burnt

No matter how many times we pop a bag of popcorn in the microwave, from time to time even if we use the same brand and the same setting with the same microwave, some of the popcorn is going to get burned. There are times in our Christian walk as we worship, work, or just fellowship with others, we can get burned. Church, work, or just life is hard by itself but when you combine all the different personalities and backgrounds, there will always come a time when someone gets burned.

It is easy to tell when popcorn is burned, because instead of a mouth-watering aroma of buttery popcorn filling the house, you get a stench that just won't go away. Even now just thinking about burnt popcorn, can cause you to make a face; I know I am.

As we walk through this life, we will encounter people that are burnt and if we are not careful, they can put a damper on us as well. Burnt people can put a bad taste in your mouth and smell up an environment, just like a bag of burnt popcorn.

Have you ever looked in the bag of overcooked popcorn? Generally, not all the pieces are burnt but even the good pieces will have some discoloration. So, even if the whole bag isn't burnt, each piece in the bag can be affected.

I know when I have a bad day, or someone hurts my feelings; I tend to let my feelings override my head. I can begin to have a negative effect on others around me, whether I mean to or not. Just like when you burn popcorn, it can affect the whole bag.

As children of the Highest, we are called to be a sweet aroma lifting up to God. None of us want to stink in the nostrils of our Saviour because of our bad attitudes. Don't get me wrong we all have bad days, or bad moments, but it is important to not let one bad situation turn into a bad week, a bad month, or especially a bad lifetime. We all get our feelings hurt, we all become tired at some point, and we all struggle, but that doesn't mean we are required to share it with anyone that will listen and create an environment that is burnt. We must continuously evaluate our attitudes and our hearts.

We need to pay attention to how others are being affected by our attitude. We should be a light in a dark world, but negativity can cause our lights to be dimmed. We need to take time each day with the Lord and ask Him to show us where we may be getting a little burnt. Allow the Holy Spirit to move in your heart so you can be a sweet savor unto the Lord.

Weekly Reflection

FOR WE ARE UNTO GOD A SWEET SAVOUR OF CHRIST, IN THEM THAT ARE SAVED, AND IN THEM THAT PERISH: 2 CORINTHIANS 2:15

Is there anything in your life that is not pleasing to the Lord? Are you holding on to a negative attitude over something that has happened? Take time to give it all to God, allow Him to minister to your heart and restore you to a sweet savour for Him.

BE YE THEREFORE FOLLOWERS OF GOD, AS DEAR CHILDREN; AND WALK IN LOVE, AS CHRIST ALSO HATH LOVED US, AND HATH GIVEN HIMSELF FOR US AN OFFERING AND A SACRIFICE TO GOD FOR A SWEET SMELLING SAVOUR. EPHESIANS 5:1-2

We are called to love others, even those who have hurt us, just as Christ loved and loves us even when we are a little burnt. Is there someone you need to show the love of Christ to?

LET ALL BITTERNESS, AND WRATH, AND ANGER, AND CLAMOUR, AND EVIL SPEAKING, BE PUT AWAY FROM YOU, WITH ALL MALICE: AND BE YE KIND ONE TO ANOTHER, TENDERHEARTED, FORGIVING ONE ANOTHER, EVEN AS GOD FOR CHRIST'S SAKE HATH FORGIVEN YOU. EPHESIANS 4:31-32

For us to be tenderhearted, we need to make sure we do not become bitter. Search your heart for any place you may have allowed a hurtful situation to turn into bitterness.

HE HATH SHEWED THEE, O MAN, WHAT [IS] GOOD; AND WHAT DOTH THE LORD REQUIRE OF THEE, BUT TO DO JUSTLY, AND TO LOVE MERCY, AND TO WALK HUMBLY WITH THY GOD? MICAH 6:8

Take some time to offer up a beautiful praise to the Father for all His loving kindness. Allow your praise to be a sweet smell unto the Lord.

Seeds

In every bag of popcorn, you get a variety of fully popped, half popped, and then those ornery little seeds that just stay hard. They refuse to pop at all and usually fall to the bottom of the bag. You know those pieces that about break your teeth if you accidently put one in your mouth. These small kernels are exposed to the same environment as all the other kernels but refuse to pop. For some reason, these kernels stay just as hard and untouched as if they had never left the shelf.

There are people in this world that hear the gospel but never let it in. They may go to church, attend studies or gospel concerts, yet never surrender their life to the One True God. They think the music is nice, the sermon was inspiring but for some unknown reason, they leave just as they came, un-popped. Maybe some feel they are good enough on their own, or someday they will think about it but right now they want to live their way.

Whatever the reason, they simply hear the word but never come out of their shell. I would like to say they are content to stay as they are, but I don't think that is the reason.

How sad to never experience God's amazing grace. You see, God doesn't just take your present life, but He takes your past, your failures, your heartache and so much more. When we surrender all to Christ, He changes you from the inside out.

A corn kernel only pops when the heat from the environment around it and in it gets so overwhelming that it can no longer sustain its current state. Each dried kernel of popcorn has a small droplet of water inside and when it is heated; it turns to steam and builds pressure. When the pressure inside can no longer be contained, it pops.

The day I gave my life to Jesus that is exactly what happened to me. The Holy Spirit was so strong and overwhelming when Jesus saved me that I felt like I was going to "pop." The hole in my soul that only God could fill was overflowing that day with His love and forgiveness. There was no way I could sit there and stay the same. I had to fall before Jesus and give it all to Him to use and change however He saw fit. I simply burst out of the rough hard shell that had once held me bound.

The hard shell is what binds us. The world holds us tight into the doubts and fears of life but surrendering to Jesus gives us freedom to live fully popped. We do not have to stay dry and thirsty; Christ gave His life so we could have a more abundant life filled with hope.

Do you feel trapped going through the motions but never really seeing a change in your heart or life? Have you heard about this Jesus but for some reason you just pushed it off and went back to life as the world calls normal? You don't have to stay there! Jesus died on a cross for all. He desires to be your Saviour and Lord of your life. Call on Jesus to set you free from that hard shell that is keeping you bound.

Have you fully surrendered your life to Christ? Have you acknowledged that Jesus Christ is your Lord and Saviour? Think about that for a moment... we often want Him as our Saviour, but we struggle with allowing Him to be Lord, but He must be both.

BUT GROW IN GRACE, AND [IN] THE KNOWLEDGE OF OUR LORD AND SAVIOUR JESUS CHRIST. TO HIM [BE] GLORY BOTH NOW AND FOREVER. AMEN. 2 PETER 3:18
Are you growing in grace? Are you going through the motions but not truly letting the Holy Spirit change your heart?

A NEW HEART ALSO WILL I GIVE YOU, AND A NEW SPIRIT WILL I PUT WITHIN YOU: AND I WILL TAKE AWAY THE STONY HEART OUT OF YOUR FLESH, AND I WILL GIVE YOU A HEART OF FLESH. EZEKIEL 36:26
Life can make us develop a very hard shell, just like the popcorn kernel, but God has promised us a new heart, a heart of flesh. I lived most of my life with a heart of stone and felt justified because of all the hurt, but when I gave my life to Jesus, oh, what a difference He has made in my heart. Ask Jesus to change your heart?

Just as God put the small drop of water inside each kernel, God has placed forever in our hearts. This means that we have a longing for eternity, but this longing can only be filled when the Holy Spirit tugs at our hearts and we accept the invitation to give our lives to   Christ.
The kernel pops and our lives are never the same. If you have never asked the Lord to forgive you of your sins and live in your heart, now, would be the perfect time. If you have given your life to Christ, take a moment   and   thank   Him.

Half Popped

Generally, in a bag of popcorn, most of the bag is only half popped. You know the ones that look fluffy but when you bite into them, they still have a little hard piece of the kernel attached. These pieces are not quite all done.

Half popped popcorn reminds me of people that say they love God but don't think you need to go overboard with this whole "religion" thing. They are content to compartmentalize their lives into sections but feel no need to fully live for Jesus. Half popped people spend time rationalizing why they don't have time to read their bibles, pray, or reach out to others. They rarely have space for quiet time or bible study yet, it is easy for them to occupy their evening with their favorite shows because they need to unwind. Their schedules can easily become too full for the things of Jesus.

I believe half popped Christians have great intentions, but for some reason, they never truly surrender everything to God. When we live a segregated life; church, work, home... we become pulled in all directions putting us only partially in everything, but the Lord wants all of us, all the time. Regardless of where we are or what we are doing, God wants it all.

I'm not sure why anyone would settle for only occasionally feeling His presence, when He has promised to be with us always. It seems insane to me to settle for half, when He has promised us the full.

Only when we learn to be fully popped for God can we have peace in all circumstances. Half-popped Christians simply don't understand how much more there is when we live surrender to Jesus all the time.

Fully surrendering and trusting the Lord only happens when we begin to know Him, and we can't possibly understand the fullness of His love, if we don't spend time with Him. Reading our Bible is like reading a great love letter from the creator of the world to each of us. Spending time reading, praying, allowing the Spirit to move in our lives is the only way to grow in faith and when we grow in faith, we begin to trust who the Lord is and believe all His promises.

God never intended for us to be half popped. He wants all of us, for all of Him. We will never arrive this side of heaven to our full potential, but we should always be growing closer to the one who gave everything for us. Are you living half popped?

Weekly Reflection

Is there a part of your life that you haven't fully surrendered to God? Are you living half popped, trying to be satisfied? Spend some time in prayer letting Him speak to your heart.

TASTE AND SEE THAT THE LORD IS GOOD: BLESSED IS THE MAN THAT TRUSTETH IN HIM. PSALM 34:8
Take God up on His word, take some time this week to experience Him in all areas of your life. Write down how it changes your day. (Ideas: start with prayer, read 5 minutes from scripture, sing praise, sit in His presence...)

VERILY, VERILY, I SAY UNTO YOU, EXCEPT A CORN OF WHEAT FALL INTO THE GROUND AND DIE, IT ABIDETH ALONE: BUT IF IT DIE, IT BRINGETH FORTH MUCH FRUIT. JOHN 12:24
When we die to ourselves, it allows us to be open to bear fruit for the Lord. Is there a part of you that needs to be opened to the Lord?

AND TO KNOW THE LOVE OF CHRIST, WHICH PASSETH KNOWLEDGE, THAT YE MIGHT BE FILLED WITH ALL THE FULNESS OF GOD. NOW UNTO HIM THAT IS ABLE TO DO EXCEEDING ABUNDANTLY ABOVE ALL THAT WE ASK OR THINK, ACCORDING TO THE POWER THAT WORKETH IN US, EPHESIANS 3:19-20

Why settle for only part when God has promised to fill us to the full? Allow the love of God to fill you to overflow in every area of your life! Don't try to rationalize and understand it but surrender all to Him! Live in His abundance today!

Fully Popped

Would it not be great to make a bag of popcorn and not have a single kernel left un-popped and not only no kernels, but each and every piece be fully popped without any shell left? In comparing a bag of popcorn with believers, it would be wonderful to say every child of God is completely devoted to living fully surrendered to the Lord, but that wouldn't be accurate.

I would be overjoyed to exclaim that all Christians live in one mind and one accord, that we are all sold out for the cause of Christ but that would not be true. Just like the bag of popcorn, life encompasses a wide range of people with different heart conditions. Some are hard, some are trying to find their way, others live life thinking a little dab will do, and then there are the ones that are burnt, but there is one more piece in the bag that we can't overlook, the fully popped kernel. The people that are completely sold out, serving the Lord and wholeheartedly want to praise the one Most High that has delivered them.

Wholehearted individuals are what I like to refer to as fully popped. Now, don't get me wrong they are not perfect, and they are not better than anyone else, but they are choosing every single day to live more like Christ and allowing Him to lead the way. Fully popped kernels have come to a place in their walk where they recognize that they can do nothing on their own and that they need the full power of the Holy Spirit moving in them to bring honor to God. They realize that their purpose is to worship and glorify the King of Kings and Lord of Lords!

Living fully popped for the Lord has less to do with how religious we are and more to do with how willing we are to give all of our life to Christ. When we get saved the light of Christ comes to reside in us all day, every day. We need to be shining the light of Jesus everywhere we go, church, work, home... our heart for Christ should not be limited by where we are.

Part of being fully popped means praying without ceasing, being in the Word and allowing the Word to live in us, so it can be poured out to others. Living fully popped isn't in the extravagant things but is in the everyday. This may sound silly but even folding the laundry can be living fully popped if we learn to do it with a grateful heart, remembering how we are blessed with family and clothes. Fully popped simply means all things for God's glory!

I discovered, not too long ago, that they make a special type of popcorn that is supposed to have no kernels once it is cooked. Now, I have not personally tried this out to see if it is true, but the thought made me smile. I smile because one day the children of God will have the privilege to worship Jesus, face to face in the realms of glory, fully popped. There will be no more tares among the wheat but fully renewed saints of God shouting Holy, Holy, Holy is the Lord God Almighty.

While eternity is a little closer every day, we must decide each moment if we will live fully popped for Jesus while here on this earth. When we allow Christ to live in us and through us, He is glorified, and our shells will fall away allowing us to live fully popped.

I AM CRUCIFIED WITH CHRIST: NEVERTHELESS, I LIVE; YET NOT I, BUT CHRIST LIVETH IN ME: AND THE LIFE WHICH I NOW LIVE IN THE FLESH I LIVE BY THE FAITH OF THE SON OF GOD, WHO LOVED ME, AND GAVE HIMSELF FOR ME. GALATIANS 2:20

We can't live surrendered on our own, we must live by faith in the one who died for us. Christ died so we could live by and through His love. Are you living through His love today?

AND HE SAID TO [THEM] ALL, IF ANY [MAN] WILL COME AFTER ME, LET HIM DENY HIMSELF, AND TAKE UP HIS CROSS DAILY, AND FOLLOW ME. LUKE 9:23

It is not a one-time surrender but a daily act of giving our lives to Christ. Ask the Lord to teach you how to live a surrendered life for Him.

AND BE RENEWED IN THE SPIRIT OF YOUR MIND; AND THAT YE PUT ON THE NEW MAN, WHICH AFTER GOD IS CREATED IN RIGHTEOUSNESS AND TRUE HOLINESS. EPHESIANS 4:22-24

Our mind can dictate our day. What we think about most will determine our focus. Try refocusing your thoughts back to God throughout the day.

Read Mathew 13:24-30. It can get discouraging to watch others that may not truly get the amazing grace that God has so freely given. Child of God, do not get weary, pray faithfully for those around you and keep keeping on for the glory of the Father. Write out a prayer for those around you that may not understand the joy you have and ask the Lord to help you not get discouraged.

Donkeys

When we see a donkey, often we only think of a stubborn animal, but a donkey is so much more. Donkeys have several characteristics that we can relate to in our lives; many of which can help us grow in our faith walk. Over the next few weeks, we will look at the different characteristics of a donkey and what scripture has to say about these characteristics.

Now, I'm not calling anybody a donkey, but if you find some areas in your life that are lining up with the lessons, say, "Oh Me!" and pray. If someone you know comes to mind during a lesson you can shout, "Amen!" and pray for them. Either way, you will forever see donkeys in a whole new light.

Strong and Smart

Donkeys are very strong animals with an incredible memory. For example, a donkey's strength can exceed that of a horse of equal size, and they have a unique ability to remember places they have traveled for up to twenty-five years. In the Old Testament donkeys were used to carry supplies for travel. The donkey's strength allowed them to bear the burden through the journey ahead while their memory allowed them to recall the worn paths they had traveled before.

We often attribute strength and memory as wonderful characteristics, but each one can be a hindrance if not used wisely. When we work in our own strength, we can become overwhelmed by the weight of life. Just like the donkey, we can end up carrying a weight that is not ours. Over time we can start to tell ourselves, "We got this!" but the problem is we don't "got this."

God tells us to lay down our heavy burdens. So, why are we trying to carry them? We are supposed to let go of the past, not hold on to it. God desires for us to cast our cares on Him and let Him sustain us. Once we surrender our lives to Christ, our past is under the blood, so stop trying to wash it off and pull it back out.

The world would like us to believe that our faith makes us weak, but the truth is, it makes us wise. No one would choose to carry their luggage on a trip if they had the means to load it in a car and drive it there. Yet, for some unknown reason, we believe we are showing our strength by carrying our burdens, past and present.

Is that you? Are you exhausted because you are wanting others to see how strong you are by carrying the heavy load all on your own? If so, stop it.

Right now... STOP... Just STOP IT!
Lay it at our Savior's feet.

If you are trying to do it all and carry it all my dear sweet friend, you don't have to. Hand it all to Jesus. Lay every care, every burden, all of your past, present and future at His feet. Every time you are reminded of the past, speak truth to yourself by loudly declaring... it is already under the blood.

If the weight you are carrying is unforgiveness, then stop and ask God to help you forgive as He has forgiven you. As a child of God, we no longer have to carry it all because Jesus came and died so He could be our burden bearer. Don't fret over the weight of it all, give it to Jesus and let Him work it all out.

Weekly Reflections

Read Psalm 55:22 and Matthew 11:30. Write out the verse that is speaking to you today.

Are you carrying a burden? Have you convinced yourself that you can handle it on your own? Child of God, you don't have to handle any problem alone. You can lay every burden down at the cross and let the Lord handle it through you. List any problems you are facing and give them to God, stop carrying the load.

Are you holding on to the past, remembering that which we ought to let go? Do you hold on to old hurts or failures allowing them to weigh you down? Write it out and let Jesus mend your heart.

FOR IF YE FORGIVE MEN THEIR TRESPASSES, YOUR HEAVENLY FATHER WILL ALSO FORGIVE YOU: BUT IF YE FORGIVE NOT MEN THEIR TRESPASSES, NEITHER WILL YOUR FATHER FORGIVE YOUR TRESPASSES. MATTHEW 6:14-15
Search your heart and see if any unforgiveness is lurking. Write out what comes to mind. Allow Jesus to help you forgive so you can move forward.

BUT WITHOUT FAITH IT IS IMPOSSIBLE TO PLEASE HIM: FOR HE THAT COMETH TO GOD MUST BELIEVE THAT HE IS, AND THAT HE IS A REWARDER OF THEM THAT DILIGENTLY SEEK HIM.
HEBREWS   11:6

Trust

Donkeys have a reputation for stubbornness. This isn't to be ornery, but it is due to their highly developed sense of self-preservation which makes it difficult to force or frighten a donkey into doing something it believes to be contrary to its own best interest or safety. This self-preservation makes it rather difficult to train a donkey since you cannot force them into submission.

Training a donkey relies on words and actions. Donkeys learn by being shown what to do and learning they can trust the one who is teaching them. Only when the donkey knows they are safe, will they begin to follow commands and go somewhere they believe to be dangerous.

Now, self-preservation is great when you are on the edge of a cliff or facing a pack of wolves but when we use it to make life all about us, we get into trouble. So as a child of God, we no longer belong to ourselves but to the Lord. The great privilege to live a life which brings honor and glory to God is now ours. We should no longer be about ourselves but about our Father's business.

Like the donkey, we can get caught up in what we want and what we believe is best and completely forget God has called us to a new life. There will be times along our journey, where we don't understand what God is doing or where He is leading but it is in these times, we must decide if we are going to trust Him. Will we choose to move forward in the call, or will we be a donkey and hold tight to what we think we know?

Trusting God becomes easier as we draw closer to the Father. With each obedient step, we learn not only is God faithful, but He is trustworthy. The Bible teaches us who God is and as we learn more about this big, amazing God the more we start to trust Him. For example, if a stranger came up to you and told you to jump off a cliff, you would laugh at them and maybe reply, "After you" but when you walk with the Lord and He says jump off the cliff, you don't worry because you know, He is the one who made the cliff, and He will either catch you or teach you to fly.

The reason we fail to see big, monumental miracles today is not because God can't. It is because we fail to trust that He will. It revolves around the mentality; I know God can; but will He do it for me. It is easy to trust yourself and do what you already know you are capable of but what a boring life. The Lord is teaching me, no... God has put a burning down in my soul that there is so much more to this journey. We just have to learn to put it all out there and trust Him. The key to this kind of life is knowing the Lord in a real and personal way.

Our faith journey will become more natural to our daily lives when we confidently trust the One leading us.

Just like the donkey, we are hesitant to obey when we aren't sure if God has our best interest at heart. When we first give our lives to the Lord, we believe God and we believe He loves us, but we don't truly know Him till we get into His word. Studying the Bible allows us to learn of God's nature and start to grasp the overwhelming love He has for us. We only trust God fully when we know Him whole heartedly and then we will be able to trust beyond what we see.

Weekly Reflection

And the Lord said, Simon, Simon, behold, Satan hath desired to have you, that he may sift you as wheat: But I have prayed for thee, that thy faith fail not: and when thou art converted, strengthen thy brethren. Luke 22:31-32

Our faith will grow as we seek to know more about God. Take some time today to write down a few characteristics of God that will help you to grow in faith. (Redeemer, Protector, Creator...)

They that trust in their wealth, and boast themselves in the multitude of their riches; In God have I put my trust: I will not be afraid what man can do unto me. Psalm 56:11

But we had the sentence of death in ourselves, that we should not trust in ourselves, but in God which raiseth the dead: 2 Corinthians 1:9

Are you trusting the Lord to direct your path or are you trusting self to make it through? Write out a time in the past month that you have demonstrated your trust in God and not self.

Is there something that you feel God has been calling you to do or say but you are afraid? Have you debated over all the reasons you can't? Take time today to write out the things that have been holding you back and give them to God.

THUS SAITH THE LORD; CURSED BE THE MAN THAT TRUSTETH IN MAN, AND MAKETH FLESH HIS ARM, AND WHOSE HEART DEPARTETH FROM THE LORD. JEREMIAH 17:5

The world would have us believe that pleasing oneself or only doing what makes us happy is the way to live, but that is not what God says. Ask God to search your heart. Are there areas in your life where it is all about you? Write it down and give everything to God.

Redeemed

In the book of Exodus, God lays out all the laws for the children of Israel to follow. God spells out in great detail how they are to obey not only the ten commandments but how-to live in fellowship with Him. One of the guidelines was that all firstborn whether it was a human or an animal, belonged to God, which meant they all would need to be redeemed back to Him.

Now I want to sidetrack for just a moment and talk about the word redeem. The word redeemed can be what I refer to as a church word so I don't want to assume that everyone will grasp the depth of that word without a little clarity.

Merriam-Webster Dictionary defines it as:
Redeem:
1. to buy back: REPURCHASE
    a: to get or win back
2: to free from what distresses or harms: such as
    a: to free from captivity by payment of ransom
    b: to extricate from or help to overcome something detrimental
    c: to release from blame or debt: CLEAR
    d: to free from the consequences of sin

You see, when Adam and Eve sinned in the garden, it birthed a nature of sin into each of us. We all have sinned and can therefore no longer stand before a Holy God. God designed us to be with Him. He created us to worship Him for eternity, but sin changed that. Yet God loved us so much that He made a way for us to be bought back (redeemed) to Him.

I know you are saying, "what does this have to do with a donkey?!" Hold on, this is where it gets good. In Exodus 34:20 it states, "The firstborn of a donkey you shall redeem with a lamb, or if you will not redeem it, you shall break its neck." Donkeys could not be redeemed by a donkey they could only be redeemed by a lamb. Are you with me? God has stated that everything that is the first is His. The first seeds from the harvest, the first fruit from the trees and the first born of all the animals belonged to God.

God makes no exceptions to His law... All must be redeemed including the donkey or there is a penalty of death.

Way too often, we look to other people to rescue us. We look to others to find our value or make us feel some type of worth. Well, guess what? We cannot be saved by man; we can only be saved by God. There is no person that can redeem you from your sin or your past. Without a sacrifice we are held to the penalty of our sin and will have an eternal death but by redemption we can be saved.

We are the donkey. We are the property of the Lord who made us and preserves us, but because of sin, God will not, cannot accept us. So, the Lamb of God must stand in our place, or we must die eternally. Jesus is the spotless lamb that paid the price for our sins and covers our lives so we can be with Him for eternity. Jesus Christ is the only redemption for our sins. Therefore, without Christ as our Lord and Saviour, we cannot be with God. There is no redemption without the lamb and the penalty is eternal death.

The spotless Lamb, Jesus Christ, has already bled for us and made a way of redemption from the fatal curse of the law. The question is, have you accepted the payment for your sins?

Weekly Reflection

This week we will not have daily reflections, instead I want you to dig deep and be honest with yourself on where you stand with the Lord.

Have you accepted Jesus Christ as Lord of your life? Have you confessed your sins to a Holy God and asked for forgiveness? Have you turned from those sins and surrendered all to His will?

Lastly, If the answer is yes to all the above, spend this week thanking and praising God for all He has done in your life?
If you can't answer yes, today is a great day to change that.   If the Holy Spirit is moving in your heart and drawing you close. Stop right now and talk to God.
Ask Him to be Lord of your life, confess your sins and ask Him to forgive you, turn from that way of life and live for Jesus. Now, share your decision to trust God. I would love to hear about it @ FindingtheMore.org

FOR GOD SO LOVED THE WORLD, THAT HE GAVE HIS ONLY BEGOTTEN SON, THAT WHOSOEVER BELIEVETH IN HIM SHOULD NOT PERISH, BUT HAVE EVERLASTING LIFE. FOR GOD SENT NOT HIS SON INTO THE WORLD TO CONDEMN THE WORLD; BUT THAT THE WORLD THROUGH HIM MIGHT BE SAVED JOHN 3:16-17

SECTION FIVE

Ants

Ants are such small, tiny creatures. We often may think of them as insignificant, yet the Lord saw fit to mention them specifically in scripture. We, too, can sometimes feel small and insignificant, yet God has specifically designed each of us for His amazing call.

Looking at the big things going on in the world around us, can make us feel pointless. We can start to wonder if we are able to make a difference.

Can I share something with you? In day-to-day life, it is the small things that make a big impact, whether we realize it or not. A simple smile, a kind word, a card, or eye contact to acknowledge you see someone can change a person's day completely.

It's the little things that change the world!

Over the next few weeks we are going to learn some attributes of the ant that the body of Christ should consider. We are going to be looking at the ant colony from the perspective of the church, but the same principles could be applied to the workplace or even the family unit.

One Accord

An average ant colony can have 60,000 to 90,000 ants. The interesting part is that each ant has a duty, and each one works according to their calling to care for the colony. Ants don't work for themselves or for their own gain but for the colony. Today's churches can have anywhere from ten to ten thousand in attendance on any given Sunday morning, yet even our smallest congregations struggle to unite for the cause of Christ.

The Bible declares that the children of God are to be one body, the body of Christ and we are to stay in one mind and one accord, yet this is not always the case. Might I dare say, it is less often the case than it should be.

Scripture teaches us to be in one accord. As a matter of fact, it repeats this phrase eleven times and twelve times it says we are one body. So, why aren't we working to obey the scriptures and be one? Could it be that we have listened to the world for too long, and believed the lie that it is all about us and our own needs?

The body of Christ is called to share the gospel, love one another, and bring glory to God through our praise and worship. On paper it doesn't sound that difficult but when you put our unique characteristics together in one place, it can become a big chore if we are trying to accomplish it in ourselves.

One accord does not mean we must agree on every single detail of life. It doesn't mean that we are happy with each other every single second of every day, but it does means working together for God's glory. It means agreeing that Jesus is the only way to heaven, that we cannot add or subtract from what Christ did through the cross and that the resurrected Jesus Christ is in heaven beside the Father.

The early church had all things common according to Acts 4:32. Yet we know that they came with different skills and backgrounds, so what did they have in common? Their commonality was their willingness to live surrendered to the Lord which enabled them to not worry over who brought more or who brought less because they knew it was for God's glory. Uniquely, the differences they brought in skills made them more capable to serve the kingdom.

The church needs to be more like the ants working together. Our purpose should not be to tear at each other or argue over our differences; we should foremost be the church. We should have one mind and one accord in our fellowship so others can see Jesus and come to know Him as Lord and Saviour.

Weekly Reflection

Look up Philippians 1:27, 2:2-5. Write out the verse that speaks to you most.

List three ways you can be more active in being one with the body of Christ.

SO WE, [BEING] MANY, ARE ONE BODY IN CHRIST, AND EVERY ONE MEMBERS ONE OF ANOTHER. HAVING THEN GIFTS DIFFERING ACCORDING TO THE GRACE THAT IS GIVEN TO US, WHETHER PROPHECY, [LET US PROPHESY] ACCORDING TO THE PROPORTION OF FAITH; OR MINISTRY, [LET US WAIT] ON [OUR] MINISTERING: OR HE THAT TEACHETH, ON TEACHING; OR HE THAT EXHORTETH, ON EXHORTATION: HE THAT GIVETH, [LET HIM DO IT] WITH SIMPLICITY; HE THAT RULETH, WITH DILIGENCE; HE THAT SHEWETH MERCY, WITH CHEERFULNESS. [LET] LOVE BE without DISSIMULATION. ABHOR THAT WHICH IS EVIL; CLEAVE TO THAT WHICH IS GOOD. [BE] KINDLY AFFECTIONED ONE TO ANOTHER WITH BROTHERLY LOVE; IN HONOUR PREFERRING ONE ANOTHER; ROMANS 12:5-10

List some ways you can demonstrate brotherly love.

FOR AS THE BODY IS ONE, AND HATH MANY MEMBERS, AND ALL THE MEMBERS OF THAT ONE BODY, BEING MANY, ARE ONE BODY: SO ALSO [IS] CHRIST. FOR BY ONE SPIRIT ARE WE ALL BAPTIZED INTO ONE BODY, WHETHER [WE BE] JEWS OR GENTILES, WHETHER [WE BE] BOND OR FREE; AND HAVE BEEN ALL MADE TO DRINK INTO ONE SPIRIT. FOR THE BODY IS NOT ONE MEMBER, BUT MANY.
1CORINTHIANS 12:12-14

Write how it makes you feel to know that we all can be part of the body of Christ.

Strength

Ants might be small, but they are very strong. Ants can carry anywhere from twenty to fifty times their body weight. You wouldn't think they are capable of such strength by just looking at them but if we take in consideration, the weight of the object verses the ant's small size, we would be in awe. Even though I work to increase my physical strength with exercise, I can't even imagine being able to pick up something twenty times my body weight much less carrying it somewhere.

Regardless of our physical capabilities, we all can be rather weak creatures. We have a way of making small things feel like mountains. We strain and struggle to manage our lives in our feeble bodies, thinking that it has to be that way. We like to do things ourselves and usually fail miserably or we become so weary from working so hard that we give up.

Let me share something with you, I do not like to be weak, and I sure don't like to feel small. I don't like it when people think they can overpower me or when I am made to believe I am less than. In myself, I would love nothing better than to never need any help and just take care of all things on my own, but that is not how we are designed. If I was capable of truly doing everything in my own strength, if you were capable of doing it all in your own strength, we wouldn't need a Saviour. Sure, there are people all over the world attempting to everything all on their own, but I guarantee, whether they let it show or not, they are exhausted.

Ants are rather wise creatures, they have learned that not only has God given them great strength individually, but by working together, they can move mountains, well at least an ant size mountain. When we surrendered our lives to Christ, we gained enormous strength. As children of God, we are now endowed with the strength of the Holy Spirit that has come to dwell within us. His strength allows us to face the biggest giants or mountains without fear.

When we face challenges as children of God, we do not have to worry about the strength of the enemy. We just have to remember the strength and power of God. The Lord teaches us that when we are His, we need only stand firm for He will fight for us. Jesus has already won the victory through the cross and resurrection, so we don't have to be at war.

I have learned that when I face defeat, it usually comes because I attempted to do it in my own strength rather than take it to the Lord and let Him fight for me.

Part of an ant's strength is understanding they need help to lift the big things. The Bible speaks of the children of God coming together to pray for boldness and power to share the gospel. They leaned on one another to keep going forward when they were being mistreated and even beaten.

We need to learn to help strengthen those around us through the Holy Spirit that lives within us. We need to remember that it is okay to be weak within ourselves if we are trusting in God for our strength. Remember God gives us strength for the day, and He always has more to give for tomorrow. So, let us not do things within our own power but in the strength of the Lord knowing that He alone can sustain us.

Jesus in the Everyday

Weekly Reflection

THEREFORE, I TAKE PLEASURE IN INFIRMITIES, IN REPROACHES, IN NECESSITIES, IN PERSECUTIONS, IN DISTRESSES FOR CHRIST'S SAKE: FOR WHEN I AM WEAK, THEN AM I STRONG. 2 CORINTHIANS 12:10
We rarely look at our difficulties as an opportunity for God's strength to shine in our lives. How can understanding this truth change your perspective on things you may be enduring?

Look up Psalm 73:26, Isaiah 40:29 and Ephesians 6:10. Write out the verse that's most encouraging to you today and repeat it back to yourself throughout the day.

BECAUSE THE FOOLISHNESS OF GOD IS WISER THAN MEN; AND THE WEAKNESS OF GOD IS STRONGER THAN MEN.
1 CORINTHIANS 1:25

THE LORD SHALL FIGHT FOR YOU, AND YE SHALL HOLD YOUR PEACE. EXODUS 14:14
I am so thankful that even God's weakness is stronger than we could ever be. What battle are you trying to fight in your own strength rather than giving it to God to fight for you?

IRON SHARPENETH IRON; SO A MAN SHARPENETH THE COUNTENANCE OF HIS FRIEND. PROVERBS 27:17

CONFESS [YOUR] FAULTS ONE TO ANOTHER, AND PRAY ONE FOR ANOTHER, THAT YE MAY BE HEALED. THE EFFECTUAL FERVENT PRAYER OF A RIGHTEOUS MAN AVAILETH MUCH. JAMES 5:16

WE THEN THAT ARE STRONG OUGHT TO BEAR THE INFIRMITIES OF THE WEAK, AND NOT TO PLEASE OURSELVES. ROMANS 15:1

Who in your life could use some encouragement or borrowed strength? What areas in your life could you use some extra strength? Write out your responses and then reach out to a brother or sister.

Work with Purpose

Ants are very unique creatures in that they all work with a purpose. The purpose being to work and sacrifice for the colony. Ants don't stress over who sees them working, they don't give up because no one said thank you or bragged about what a wonderful job they did, and ants don't change colonies if they don't move up in rank. Ants realize that they are all important and it takes all of them to keep the colony going. Guess what child of God? Every Christian is important to the church.

In a colony of ants there is a division of labor. Each ant has a specific job they are born into, and they work diligently at that job without complaint of, "Why do I have to do this job?" Ants understand that for the colony to thrive every job must be accomplished and that it takes all of them working toward the purpose of the colony to succeed. As Christians, we must not labor for ourselves but ask, "How I can use the skills that God has given me to bring Him honor and further the kingdom of God?"

Ants don't fight over needing a new job with more importance because they know every job is important in the colony. The world tells us that some jobs are more important than others and if you don't have a visible position, you must be low in the ranks. Truth is, some of the most rewarding and impactful jobs are the ones no one ever sees. Prayer warriors are extremely important to the body of Christ and only God will ever know the time and energy spent calling out to Him.

No job is insignificant in the body of Christ. For example, I'm not a good greeter, small talk is exhausting, and hugs are not my thing. Yes, I'm slowly coming around to hugs when nudged by the Holy Spirit, but in general, I'm not good at the outward compassion area. But God has placed wonderfully gifted people in our congregation that are amazing at greeting, they never meet a stranger, they love small talk and enjoy shaking hands and hugging necks. When you put as all together, we are one body serving with purpose.

If we, alone, try to do all the jobs, we can become overwhelmed and exhausted, but if we each do the job we are called to, we will thrive for the glory of God, and all will be accomplished because no one will be working to do someone else's task rather than the one God has for them. As the body of Christ, we need to be a colony, working together for the purpose of His kingdom because we are His people.

This devotional has looked at the colony from the perspective of the church, but everyone that has accepted Jesus Christ as Lord and Saviour is a part of this body. All of us make up His colony. Therefore, we must not only use our callings in the church but in our communities, on our jobs, and within our families. Our purpose should reach beyond our church communities, but in that we must be careful to not neglect the importance of the church.

Weekly Reflection

Take time to look up and write out 2 Corinthians 9:7 and ask God to show you if there is any area of ministry that you have a grudging spirit toward.

Are you always trying to do it all? Ask God to show you what you may be trying to do that someone else can help with or even take over because He didn't call you to it.

Have you sat down on the Lord because you want to do something else rather than what He has called you to do? Have you allowed others to make you feel inadequate to accomplish what Jesus has called you to? Take some time and write out what's on your heart.

God has created us all with purpose, the purpose to serve one another and build up the kingdom of God. Our purpose as the church is to draw others to Him. The work God has called you to, will give you a sense of purpose. Write out Romans 8:28.

Help!

We have already looked at how ants work with one purpose, but ants also look out for one another. Ants have the ability to secrete pheromones to send out a message to other ants. These pheromones are used to let others know where food is and if an ant is hurt.

Forgers in a colony go out and scout surrounding areas for food. When food is found, they secrete a special pheromone letting the other ants know that they have found food. An interesting fact, ants have two stomachs. They use one stomach to feed themselves and the second stomach holds food to share with the other ants. By having two stomachs, an ant is able to care for themselves and care for the ants that stay behind to work for the queen and the colony. If we could take this process and apply it to our community, how amazing would it be.

The world around us teaches us to hold tight to all that we have. We are taught to fear sharing with others because if we give any away, we might not have enough for ourselves. This mentality can make us weary about giving, or even worse, cause us to only share what is left over.

God doesn't want us to share only crumbs. He wants us to call everyone to the table and if they can't get there, then we should take it to them.

We need to be more ant minded and be more open to searching out and helping those in need. We are usually good at reaching out to help our brothers and sisters when we are asked or when a need is made known to us, but that requires people to ask. How about the people in need that don't know where to reach out or who to ask for help? Are we putting ourselves out there to let those in need know we are willing to help? Like the ant releases pheromones to let the others know, "Hey, there is food over here!", do we call out to one another? Try putting yourself out there and telling others you are willing to help.

I understand that we may not be in a position to help everyone, or we might not even know how to help in some situations, but we all can pray for one another and walk beside each other to find the help someone needs. Such as, I might not be in a position to feed your family for a week, but I can help with a meal and reach out to others to join in and help. I might not be able to buy a coat for all the people in my town, but I can buy what I am able to with what God has blessed me with and help as many as possible. If each of us would do what we can, God will honor our efforts and multiply the blessing.

When an ant gets hurt, they are able to use a different scent to let others know they are injured. When the pheromone is released, the other ants will find the ant by following the scent and carry them back to care for them. Can I say that this would be so beneficial in ministry! People get upset because no one checked on them or came to see them while they were sick, but the problem with that is... they never told anyone they were hurt.

As the body of Christ, when one is hurt, we are all affected. We need to learn to reach out, send a signal, so others know to come and help and if need be, carry us to safety. We can't sit on the side of the deserted road wounded and just expect others to know where to find us.

When we find ourselves hurt, we need to first call out to Jesus. We need to let Him be the great physician in our lives and then we should reach out to our brothers and sisters and allow them to help us in our time of crisis. We are all called to be the hands and feet of Jesus but that can be difficult if we don't know. Reach out, it's okay to need help, and it is okay to just want someone to sit with you while you recover. So, be like the ant and call out!

Weekly Reflection

BUT BY AN EQUALITY, [THAT] NOW AT THIS TIME YOUR ABUNDANCE [MAY BE A SUPPLY] FOR THEIR WANT, THAT THEIR ABUNDANCE ALSO MAY BE [A SUPPLY] FOR YOUR WANT: THAT THERE MAY BE EQUALITY: 2 CORINTHIANS 8:14

Do you have more than enough? Has God blessed you with an abundance of something? Take an assessment of something you can share with others, maybe it's an extra coat or pair of shoes or maybe it is an abundance of joy that you can share to encourage others. List out what God puts on your heart, we all have something to give.

OPEN THY MOUTH, JUDGE RIGHTEOUSLY, AND PLEAD THE CAUSE OF THE POOR AND NEEDY. PROVERBS 31:9

DEFEND THE POOR AND FATHERLESS: DO JUSTICE TO THE AFFLICTED AND NEEDY. PSALM 82:3

In what ways can you reach out to the poor and needy in your community?

BUT WHOSO HATH THIS WORLD'S GOOD, AND SEETH HIS BROTHER HAVE NEED, AND SHUTTETH UP HIS BOWELS [OF COMPASSION] FROM HIM, HOW DWELLETH THE LOVE OF GOD IN HIM? MY LITTLE CHILDREN, LET US NOT LOVE IN WORD, NEITHER IN TONGUE; BUT IN DEED

AND IN TRUTH. AND HEREBY WE KNOW THAT WE ARE OF THE TRUTH, AND SHALL ASSURE OUR HEARTS BEFORE HIM.
1 JOHN 3:17-19

While you were reading this verse or when you read the devotion, did a certain person come to your mind? Did you see the face of a brother or sister that is in need that maybe you haven't reached out to? If so, write out a prayer for how God would have you help them and if no one came to mind ask God to show you someone that needs help that you can reach out to.

BEAR YE ONE ANOTHER'S BURDENS, AND SO FULFIL THE LAW OF CHRIST. GALATIANS 6:2

CONFESS YOUR FAULTS ONE TO ANOTHER, AND PRAY ONE FOR ANOTHER, THAT YE MAY BE HEALED. THE EFFECTUAL FERVENT PRAYER OF A RIGHTEOUS MAN AVAILETH MUCH. JAMES 5:16

Do you have a need that you have been struggling with? Are you afraid to reach out for help or even ask for prayer from others? Let today be the day it changes. Write out why you haven't shared the need and put in God's hands. Ask God to show you who to reach out to.

GO TO THE ANT, THOU SLUGGARD; CONSIDER HER WAYS, AND BE WISE: WHICH HAVING NO GUIDE, OVERSEER, OR RULER, PROVIDETH HER MEAT IN THE SUMMER, [AND] GATHERETH HER FOOD IN THE HARVEST. PROVERBS 6:6-8

SECTION SIX

❋

Storms

Storms can be beautifully amazing events to behold, especially, when you are in a safe place, but that same storm can be terrifying when you are stuck in it, with no protection in sight. As a child, my grandmother would make everyone go down to the basement any time a storm came calling. She would barely raise the garage style door on the basement drive and have us sit quietly till the storm passed. My grandmother would tell us God was angry, so we needed to be still and quiet.

As a grownup, I wonder if she really believed God was angry or maybe she just needed some silence since she wasn't used to having people in the house. Either way, I gained a healthy respect for storms at a young age.

Storms can come without warning and leave a mark. They can be destructive and nourishing all at the same time. The wind can take down trees and blow debris everywhere, while the rain feeds the plants and fills the waterways with refreshment.

Every storm is not bad, but we must take assessment of what kind of storm we are in. It can be fun to dance in the rain or splash in a few mud puddles, especially if you have on rain boots, but it's not so fun to play in a hurricane where you can be swept away or taken down by flying tree branches.

The next few weeks, we will look at four types of storms. Each storm can be a bit overwhelming to face but be encouraged, in the midst of them all, the creator of the storm is with us.

When Jesus Places Us in the Storm

There will be times when God sends us out in a storm. The thought of this may paralyze us with fear, but God does not place us there to frighten us but rather, to build our faith.

In verse 35 of Mark chapter 4, we learn of an evening when Jesus looked at His disciples and told them to get into a boat; they were going to the other side. It is important to remember that Jesus tells them to get into the boat and it is just as important to acknowledge that He has declared unto them that they are going to the other side.

You see, we will all face times when the Lord will send us out on the waters. The waters may be calm, or they could become rough and stormy, but we must trust that either way, God knew what was coming before He sent us out. We must remember that He has a purpose for putting us in the storm whether we understand it or not. Our job is to trust God and His divine faithfulness in all circumstances.

Storms can make us begin to waver or doubt if we heard Jesus correctly. The devil may come along and say, "Did God really tell you to get in the boat?" Or "If God cared about you, He wouldn't have put you in this boat." but during these times we must hold true to His calling, trusting that if we are living surrendered to God's will, there is safety, even in the storm.

Verse 37 says a storm arose and pounded waves into the ship to the point that it was full, yet Jesus slept. I wonder sometimes if the disciples were so panicked by their circumstances that they forgot Jesus told them they were going to the other side?

Aren't we the same when we allow the world to get us so overwhelmed with all the things of this life that we forget that Jesus is with us? We forget that Jesus has promised us peace unlike anything this world can offer. He has told us if we have accepted Him as Lord and Saviour, we are going to the other side. Yet, there are days where we get so involved in the world's problems, all we see is the sinking ship wondering where God went, when all along He is with us in the boat.

The disciples finally wake the Master in a panic, accusing Him of not caring but Jesus in all His love and mercy gets up and speaks to the winds and the waves, "Peace be still." (Mark 4:39) As calm fell on the waters, the disciples were exceedingly fearful. They had seen the miracles, his healing power, how spirits obeyed when He called them out, but now to see that even creation obeyed when He spoke... Who is this Jesus?

Today, we get the advantage of being able to read the full counsel of God in the Bible, so it seems unfair to judge how the people of scripture responded but it can help us decide how we will respond. What if the disciples would have called out to Jesus right when the wind picked up? Have you ever thought about that?

Are you in the middle of a storm? Have you called out to the Master for help or are you going to wait till your ship is full and going down? Remember, Jesus is always with you, so don't wait till you are drowning to cry out to Him. Call on Jesus today and let Him speak to the storm (s) in your life.

Weekly Reflection

Have you been obedient to the call on your life, yet you feel like you are in the middle of a storm? Remember even in the storm, He is still God, and He is with you. Read Mark 4:35-41, write down anything that sticks out to you.

"THEN THEY CRY UNTO THE LORD IN THEIR TROUBLE, AND HE BRINGETH THEM OUT OF THEIR DISTRESSES. HE MAKETH THE STORM A CALM, SO THAT THE WAVES THEREOF ARE STILL." PSALM 107:28-29
Is there something troubling you? Are you facing a distress that seems too overwhelming? Share it with Jesus.

Luke 8:22-25 tells of the same account, read this passage and see if something different speaks to you.

"TEACHING THEM TO OBSERVE ALL THINGS WHATSOEVER I HAVE COMMANDED YOU: AND, LO, I AM WITH YOU ALWAY, [EVEN] UNTO THE END OF THE WORLD. AMEN." MATTHEW 28:20
Looking back, is there a storm from your past that Jesus allowed you to go through to build your faith? Write down how being in the storm grew your faith

JESUS WAS WITH HIS DISCIPLES THROUGH-OUT THE STORM AND HE IS WITH US IN OUR STORMS. THE DEVIL WOULD LIKE NOTHING BETTER THAN FOR US TO BELIEVE THAT WE ARE ALL ALONE WHEN THE WIND AND WAVES SEEM TOO POWERFUL BUT WE ARE NEVER ALONE AND WE ARE NOT MEANT TO FACE THE STORM IN OUR STRENGTH BUT HIS, FOR HE HAS PROMISED WE ARE GOING TO THE OTHER SIDE.

When the Storm Rages On

This week's storm, no one is ever excited about. We like to see Jesus stepping out and calming the storm; we like to see creation obey His powerful presence but what do we do when He allows the storm to rage on? When we pray for God to calm the storm, we are asking for a reprieve from our circumstances, but God puts us in these circumstances to grow our faith. So, there will be times that the storm well keep raging on.

In Matthew 14:22-33, we see where Jesus once again sends the disciples out on a boat, but this time He stays behind to pray. Just as before, a storm brews out on the water and the disciples become fearful. This time Jesus comes walking on the water and when the disciples see this figure on the water, they become even more afraid. Jesus then speaks to them to calm their fears. When Peter realizes that it is Jesus, he asks to come out on the water.

Side note Peter gets a bad rap for sinking and for taking his eyes off of Jesus but let me clarify that he wasn't the only disciple in the boat and no one else had faith enough to ask to walk on water or to even say, "I'm next!" It took a deep trust in Christ for Peter to believe that he could walk on the water at Jesus' allowance. So, let's not throw stones!

The disciples were everyday people just like us, they could do amazing things through faith, but they were human beings that move, breathe, and think just like we do. So, when I look at this account, I sit and ponder our last devotion. Back in Matthew 8:23-27, we see where Jesus spoke, "Peace be still" and part of me wonders if Peter believed that Jesus would calm the storm when he stepped out on the water? After all, that is what Jesus had done last time. During the first storm Jesus spoke peace to nature, but this time Jesus had something else in mind.

Jesus allowed Peter to come out on the water and he was doing well until he noticed the storm wasn't stopping. He got to looking at how big the waves were and started to let fear overtake him. At that moment Peter began to sink; however, Peter also knew where his help would come from and called out to Jesus to save him.

I love how Matthew 14:31 declares, "And immediately Jesus stretched forth [His] hand, and caught him," Jesus didn't let him fall far but he let him stay in the storm. Jesus calmed Peter in the storm's midst rather than stilling the raging waters. Uniquely enough, Jesus waits till they are back in the boat to calm the storm.

There is a southern gospel song by the McKameys entitled "He Calms Me" which says, "sometimes He calms the storm and sometimes He calms me." How true.

Some storms grow our trust in Jesus; to help us learn to rely on Him in the midst of the storm. When the Lord provides for us in the middle of the storm keeping us safe, allowing us to praise Him regardless of our circumstances, we can glorify Him to the world. Others will not understand how we can have such peace while facing such hardships. This allows us the opportunity to tell everyone that it is all by faith in Jesus.

Read Matthew 14:22-32. What stands out to you in these verses? Do you relate to Peter or the other disciples? Why?

Jesus will rescue you in the storm when you call, but He will not always take you out of the storm. Read the verse below and allow it to sink in; Jesus not only calms our hearts but our minds. Ask God to give you peace in whatever you may be facing today even if your circumstances do not change.

"AND THE PEACE OF GOD, WHICH PASSETH ALL UNDERSTANDING, SHALL KEEP YOUR HEARTS AND MINDS THROUGH CHRIST JESUS". PHILIPPIANS 4:7

Where in your life can you allow God to be your refuge from the storm?

Look up Isaiah 43:2. This verse does not say God will keep you from the waters but that the Lord will be with you through it all. He will not allow us to be overtaken. Spend some time in praise knowing that even in the storm, God is good.

When the Storm is for Others

As much as we would love to believe otherwise, everything doesn't always have to do with us, disappointing right? There will be circumstances we go through in this life, so others can see the amazing provision of God. During these times, we can remember how amazing our God is and trust Him with the outcome by gracefully going through the storm or we can moan and groan complaining the whole time never allowing His glory to be revealed.

In Acts 27:18-36, another big storm comes to call while on a ship, but this time before setting sail, Paul tried to tell the people that it would not end well, but they decided to sail anyway not listening to Paul. This particular storm was so intense scripture tells us they were not only tossed by the waves, but they had started to lighten the load on the ship trying to survive.

They first got rid of everything not attached to the ship, but as the storm continued to beat down on them, they began to even tear the ship apart to lighten the load in hopes that they would not perish. I've never been in that position, but I'm pretty sure if I'm desperate enough to deconstruct the ship keeping me above water, it must be a really rough storm.

If you are a child of God, there are people all around you with no hope, they are tossing everything overboard in desperation to survive. They are even willing to toss out their values and all they hold dear in an attempt to stay afloat.

Verse 20 states they had not seen the sun, moon, or stars for many days. The men on this boat were not only in darkness but had no clue which direction they were going or how to get back on course. Any of this sound familiar? The world is looking frantically, whether they acknowledge it or not, for someone or something to show them the way, to lead them to hope and encouragement but all they see is the dark. It is our job to be light, to show them there is a way out of the darkness, a way through the storm.

Paul was right in the middle of all this chaos but without despair. Paul stood up in the middle of the storm and told all the men that God had sent an angel to let him know that other than the ship, all would survive. You see, God had a plan for Paul's life and in God's great love, spared all those who were with Paul on the ship.

The Lord may put people in your life who are difficult, He may put you in a workplace where you are surrounded by others that have no clue who Jesus is or that salvation is possible for them. This is where you can be the light in the middle of the storm. This is where you can shine through the clouds and torrential rain that is blinding those around you.

Paul not only endured the storm but had to give up the security of the ship and jump in the waters with the rest of the crew. When we live surrendered to the call of Christ in our lives, we must remember, He is the prize and He is the safe place for us to rest, not the securities of this world (not the ship). Our willingness to bring God glory in the storm can allow others to find the only true hope of this world, Jesus!

BE MERCIFUL UNTO ME, O GOD, BE MERCIFUL UNTO ME: FOR MY SOUL TRUSTETH IN THEE: YEA, IN THE SHADOW OF THY WINGS WILL I MAKE MY REFUGE, UNTIL [THESE] CALAMITIES BE OVERPAST. PSALM 57:1

Weekly Reflection

Read Acts 27:18-36, write down what stands out to you as you look at it with a new perspective.

AND WE KNOW THAT ALL THINGS WORK TOGETHER FOR GOOD TO THEM THAT LOVE GOD, TO THEM WHO ARE THE CALLED ACCORDING TO [HIS] PURPOSE. ROMANS 8:28

This verse has been taken out of context by many to believe that only good comes to those who believe but on the contrary, it shows that even when we are in the storm or when we lose the ship, God will work it to His glory and to the greater good. Is there something in your life right now that is difficult for you to see any good coming out of it? Can you look back from this point, on things from your past, and see how God took a difficult time and used it for good or to impact someone else's life? Write it out.

Do you know someone facing a storm similar to one you have faced before? Write out how the Lord brought you through that storm and then send them a word of encouragement by calling, texting, or mailing them a card to let them know how the Lord brought you through.

Jesus in the Everyday

LET YOUR LIGHT SO SHINE BEFORE MEN, THAT THEY MAY SEE YOUR GOOD WORKS, AND GLORIFY YOUR FATHER WHICH IS IN HEAVEN. MATTHEW 5:16

Have you been struggling with a difficult situation or environment? Sit with the Lord and ask Him how He would have you shine for Him so He can be glorified. Jot down what God speaks to your heart.

When We Create Our Own Storms

There are times in our lives that we don't like the direction in which the Lord is guiding us, so we decide to go our own way; thinking we know best, however, we must remember that the Lord's ways are not our ways. When we go in the wrong direction, God will call us back.

Do you remember Jonah in the Bible? (If not, it's okay) Maybe the name is not familiar, but you might have heard someone mention a man being swallowed by a big fish. Let's take a look at an overview.

Jonah was told to go to Nineveh and warn the people of God's upcoming punishment for their wickedness. The problem is Jonah doesn't care for the city of Nineveh and decides rather than do what God has said, he will run the other way and get on a boat. (Not sure why we ever believe that we can hide from the one who created all the earth but here we are with Jonah thinking he can hide in a boat.) As the ship heads out to sea, a storm begins to take hold of the boat and toss it all around. The men are scared and begin to cry out wondering why this terrible storm has come to destroy them. Jonah is in the center of the boat sleeping when the men come to him and ask him to cry out to his God for help. Jonah, however, knows that the storm is for him.

Child of God, we can run from God but the very space we run to is the very space He created. We can get ourselves into a mess by failing to follow God's word and we can even become comfortable enough to sleep in the midst of our mess. We may be willing to live in the midst of the storms we create until we see how our choice is affecting the people around us. Then we notice the mess we have created for them and ourselves.

The storms of our making are not to hurt us but to turn us back to Him. When we become set on doing things our own way and going our own direction, we put distance in our fellowship with God. Remember, God loves us too much to allow us to get too far from Him. In His love, He sends a storm to open our eyes, to redirect our path back to His loving care.

Are you in the middle of a storm right now? Have you cried out to the Father and still haven't seen the storm subside? Ask God to show you if this storm is of your own making? If the answer is yes, ask Him to remind you of the last thing He asked you to do or last place He told you to go.

Weekly Reflection

Take time to read Jonah 1:2-7 today. What stands out to you as you read over these verses?

At the beginning of this account, God tells Jonah where to go and what to say but Jonah decides not to listen. Is God calling you to go and tell someone about Jesus? Don't wait on the storm to come, list below ways you can be obedient today.

Can you remember a time you were in a storm of your own making? Do you recall how God brought you to the other side in love? Write out a prayer of gratitude for not letting you stray too far.

AND HE SAID UNTO THEM, TAKE ME UP, AND CAST ME FORTH INTO THE SEA; SO SHALL THE SEA BE CALM UNTO YOU: FOR I KNOW THAT FOR MY SAKE THIS GREAT TEMPEST [IS] UPON YOU. JONAH 1:12

Look closely at verse 5&6, Jonah was not the only one affected by the storm. When we choose to not follow the call of Christ in our lives, not only do we hinder ourselves, but we cause others to endure the storm. Is there someone who has been brought into a storm because of your running? Is there anybody that you need to help restore because of your disobedience?

THE STORMS OF LIFE ARE INEVITABLE BUT WHEN OUR HOPE IS IN THE MAKER OF THE STORM, THEY ARE ALWAYS BEARABLE!

Seasons

We all will face different seasons; some we enjoy and some not so much. Depending on where you live, the seasons may be subtle or very pronounced, but every season has very distinct characteristics that let you know they have arrived. Spring brings about newness, summer leads to longer days with more heat, fall brings change of colors and falling away, and winter brings a time of dormancy and a drop in temperature.

Everyone has a favorite season; one that brings you just a little bit more excitement than all the rest. You might enjoy sunshine and flip-flops, while the next person would rather have snow and a pair of boots. Regardless of which one you prefer; we all experience the beauty of each season at one time or another.

The Bible demonstrates the seasons we experience through the lives of others. For example, Elisabeth, the mother of John the Baptist, was barren for the greater portion of her life which would have felt much like winter. After the age of sixty, spring arose and she delivered a beautiful baby boy, new life. Summer appeared as she reared him up in the ways of the Lord but I'm sure all too soon for Elisabeth, John went about his calling from before his birth to prepare the way for the Saviour, fall.

In Luke chapter 8, we learn of the woman with the issue of blood. We can see the seasons in her life account. When the issue of blood came into her life it would have been fall as her life changed and things started to fall away. As the years past, her money was gone, and healing was a distant dream. The isolation must have felt like winter but then she heard news of this Jesus. Spring appeared as her hope arose that she too could be healed. After she bravely touched the hem of His garment, life was restored to her body and the bleeding stopped, she was able to experience summer, days of routine interaction with others.

As we live here on earth, we will also face the seasons of life. Some will last a few months and others may drag on for what seems like an eternity. Seasons change from life and growth, to falling away where everything seems to change, to times where things feel cold or even dead. Then, out of nowhere, new life will appear. God is the maker of all things and as He strategically set up the wonders of nature, He has also set up the seasons of our lives. So, regardless of the season we are currently facing, we can hold tight to His promises, knowing God is in full control of them all.

Summer

I'm going to start this devotion out by letting you know that I'm not a summer person. I don't care for the high temperatures and I'm definitely not about getting sand everywhere or anywhere for that matter. Yet, I know that summer is just as important to the scheme of life as spring and fall.

Summer is generally a time of sunshine, long days and more of a relaxed and steady routine. As kids we enjoy summer not only because school is out but because it can mean swimming and playing outside with your neighborhood friends. As we get older, summer is more about long days and how to stay cool without raising the power bill. Funny how our perspective changes!

For nature, summer is about the newness of spring continuing to grow into sustainable life. Welcomed thunderstorms bring refreshing rain and a drop in temperature by a few degrees. The seeds have now blossomed, and gardens are full of bounty or at least that is the hope.

The summer season of life can become routine. It is the nothing spectacular season. Family is good, work is fine, and the children are restless but excited to not be in school. Church life is nice, and drama is down. Summer can even feel like a little bit of a rut if we are not careful.

Society today is so busy, busy, busy that we can get accustomed to the madness and then when we get time to breath and focus, we become unimpressed with life. The calm of things can be slightly mundane.

Spiritually we love it when things are exciting. We love when the Spirit is moving, and lives are changing. We enjoy new ministries and being on fire for the Lord but sometimes we will go through a summer where God will let us grow in the heat. We still get up and spend time in the word each day but for this season it feels like nothing new. We pray, sing, praise but it feels a little flat or even mundane.

Child of God, this is where we need to be most faithful. We need to draw up closer to the Lord. I have found that when this type of summer comes it is usually just before a great adventure. As a child I was always ready for school to end but the last few weeks of summer were generally long and boring which made going back to school not so dreadful.

Our spiritual summer can be the same, we may welcome a few weeks of peace and calm but then we long for the excitement and overflowing of the Spirit moving through us. I find it is easy to be tuned in during seasons of drought and plenty but when it is all just smooth, I can feel a little lost. We don't know what to do with ourselves when there is nothing pressing to get done, but a time of routine is not a bad thing.

The change in seasons can make our faith walk overwhelming sometimes but that is why it is important to enjoy the summers when they come. We need to use this season to just sit with Jesus. Take time to patiently wait for the Lord to speak, move, or prepare us for what is ahead. A time to gather our energy and build our strength for what may come next.

So, while summer may not be my favorite, it is becoming a more welcomed season in which to simply learn to enjoy the routine of life. I'm welcoming the joy of sitting with Him in the beauty of creation, while the sun shines on my face. Just like the garden that grows and produces throughout the summer, I too am learning to take this time to grow in my relationship with God, so I'll be ready for harvest.

"We are not intended for the mountains, for sunrises, or the other beautiful attractions in life – those are simply intended to be moments of inspiration. We are made for the valley and the ordinary things of life and that is where we have to prove our stamina and strength." Oswald Chambers

It is in the ordinary, day in and day out, task of life that we must learn to celebrate our Lord. Take time today to praise Him for the simplicity of the mundane just like you would for the victories.

To every [thing there is] a season, and a time to every purpose under the heaven: - Ecclesiastes 3:1
God has a purpose for every season of our lives. Set aside some time for the Lord to speak to your heart about the season you are in and how to navigate this season of life.

If you follow the same routine each day for quiet time, try shaking it up a bit. I'm not referring to a new devotional but change it up. Go outside and feel the wind on your face as you thank God for the blessing of a new day. Turn up your favorite praise song, then dance and sing before the Lord. Download a Bible app that will read the word to you as you follow along. Try adding in a new time to just soak in His presence, maybe at lunch or right before you go to bed.

In Acts 3 there is a lame man that is carried daily to the gate called beautiful, to ask alms. Daily this man had to sit and beg for others to help him but what he didn't know was this day the Holy Spirit would come by his way and change his life forever. Summer seasons can seem like doing the same thing over and over without understanding why things aren't changing. Be faithful in being obedient even in the day to day because you never know when the Holy Spirit will come by and change us or someone else close to us. Read Acts 3:2-8 and be encouraged.

Fall

Fall can be a really beautiful time in nature, all the leaves start turning from green to red, yellow, and orange. The temperature becomes a little cooler making outside excursions more tolerable. For some it is the beginning of their favorite sport and tailgating. Regardless of what it is that makes you feel like fall has arrived, arrive it will.

Fall generally means a time of change for nature and us. The beautiful colors of fall not only demonstrate a time of change but also signals it's about time for them to let go and descend gracefully to the ground. This season is a time in our lives when there is a transition in some form or fashion.

Now, for some, change can be a hard thing, while others take it in stride, excited for what it can become in the future. Regardless of whether we like it or not, change is bound to come, just like fall.

Fall can come in different forms. Parents can experience it when their children decide it is time to move out or when family dynamics are no longer the same. For others, this season may start with medical or health issues no one saw coming; a diagnosis that will alter life as they know it for a time. Maybe after thirty years your job is shutting down and you must figure out what is next at a later stage of life.

As with life and nature, we can have spiritual seasons of fall where change is necessary. Maybe you have been in the same ministry since shortly after you gave your life to Christ and now you feel the Lord leading you away to something else, but He hasn't revealed to you the next step. It could be that a brother or sister in Christ that is your go to partner in ministry, gets the call to move to another state or maybe even a mission field on the other side of the world. Maybe your fall looks like a season of struggling in your faith trying to figure out the harder parts of life and how to make peace with the Saviour.

Fall isn't meant to rock our world to the point of despair. Throughout scripture the Bible teaches that God is the God of creation, He wants to do a new thing in our lives but that can only happen when we are willing to let go of a few things. We learn that old things pass away and behold all things become new and we love that all brand new, but we would like it to come without having to let go of the old.

If the tree had a voice, I'm sure it would be sad to see all of its foliage fall to the ground but I'm confident that the time of rest and relief from all that weight dropping to the ground can be refreshing at the same time.

We must let go of who we believe we are and what we think we are supposed to be doing, in order for the Lord to lead us in all the things that He has for our lives. It is okay to mourn the falling away as long as we don't long for what we use to have rather than celebrate all that the Lord is doing now. We must learn to look ahead at the beauty of where we are going which will keep us from staring at the past and what is no more.

Weekly Reflection

Is there something you are holding tight to that you know God wants you to let fall away? Trust it to God and let Him prepare you for the new thing. Read 2 Corinthians 5:17

JESUS CHRIST THE SAME YESTERDAY, AND TODAY, AND FOREVER. HEBREW 13:8
Change will come in this life, but we can be reassured by the knowledge that our God will never change. So, if it feels like the changes you are facing right now are too much, rest in the peace that our God never changes.

NOW UNTO HIM THAT IS ABLE TO KEEP YOU FROM FALLING, AND TO PRESENT YOU FAULTLESS BEFORE THE PRESENCE OF HIS GLORY WITH EXCEEDING JOY, JUDE 1:24
Just because we are in the spiritual season of fall does not mean we are going to fall. When our circumstances catch us off guard and it seems like all our leaves are falling from the tree, God still has us. The tree still

stands even though it is barren for a time. God will keep us from falling if we put our trust in Him. Spend some time in the word today allowing the Holy Spirit to minister to you.

Rather than mourn what you feel is lost in this season of change, take time and ask the Lord to begin to reveal to you and prepare you for the next season of life.

Winter

Winter is my favorite season! I know, I know there aren't too many of us out there, but we do exist. I enjoy the cold temperatures, hot drinks, and on occasion the beauty of snow fall as the ground becomes draped in a magnificent white cloak of inspiration. There is nothing more invigorating than to take in a big deep breath of winter's chilly air, that crisp aroma of snow. Not to mention, it doesn't hurt that we get to wear cuddly sweaters and boots, which can be difficult to pull off in the summer.

Nature displays the season with barren trees, empty fields and dried out grass. Birds have flown to warmer places while other animals take advantage of this time to fatten up and hibernate. The cold temperatures allow nature to sleep. Days are shorter and the stars are the brightest of the year.

Then there is the snow. Even people that don't care for the cold, can usually agree that there is something rather magical about a fresh white covered landscape, at least when it is on a small scale. There is just something peaceful and lovely about watching snow fall to the earth. To look out and find the dreary barren ground coated in a pristine blanket of snow... just beautiful.

A spiritual winter can be one of the hardest seasons to experience but can also have moments of joy like snow. Now, where I live the snow is short lived. So, while I may enjoy it, it is only a small part of winter. For most, winter is a difficult time leading to feelings of separation and/or sadness. When we are struggling spiritually, it can feel just like winter. We can start to feel isolated and alone. This is a time when it can become easy to think or ask, "Where is the Lord?" Winter may arrive when we lose a loved one or someone close to us turns away. It can become cold and dreary in our soul when we don't understand our circumstances and we feel like our questions go unanswered. We can begin to pull away when we believe we have given our all, only to find out it wasn't enough.

A spiritual winter makes me think of the death of Christ. The disciples had seen the miracles and trusted in the Son of God. Many had walked away from everything they knew. They didn't have any back up plans because they knew this Jesus was the Messiah! Then the darkest of all days came, Jesus was nailed upon a cross and died. I'm sure some of them thought, "Did we get it wrong? Why did He just leave us?" This was surely the coldest spiritual day of their lives.

When we find out some one we love has cancer or some illness, it is a difficult day. We may call out to God and ask for healing. We may watch them suffer through agonizing treatments only to find out it didn't work. Then the day comes when the battle is lost, and we experience the feeling of darkness. Our soul begins to yearn, and we can't quit see the light. Winter has come, regardless of what nature is doing, spiritually winter has come.

It is just for this reason that winter is my favorite! Because...

Winter means that Spring is coming. You see, Jesus might have died on that cross and He may have been placed in a grave which made this winter extremely hard, but what they didn't realize was that after every winter... Spring comes! For after three days the grave was opened and Jesus was resurrected! The disciples had been told what was to come but they could not wrap their minds around what Jesus was saying, they were struggling in the depths of winter at His death. How could this miracle worker, their Messiah be dead? Yet they had seen the whole thing! They had forgotten that Spring was Coming and not only for them, but this Spring meant new life for everyone that would accept Jesus as Lord and Saviour!

It may seem like a long and unbearable winter that you are walking through right now. It may feel like you will never see the sun again but hold on brother/sister because the best part of a long dark winter is the reassurance that Spring is coming.

The battle may have been lost on this side of glory but if you are a child of the King, the war has already been won and what feels like winter here is spring, new life, for our loved ones who have passed in the faith. So, don't be defeated by the winters of this life because that simply means, there is a Spring coming.

Weekly Reflection

The winter snow is a reminder to the children of God that we too are now whiter than snow by the precious blood of Jesus Christ. Write out Isaiah 1:18

FOR GOD, WHO COMMANDED THE LIGHT TO SHINE OUT OF DARKNESS, HATH SHINED IN OUR HEARTS, TO GIVE THE LIGHT OF THE KNOWLEDGE OF THE GLORY OF GOD IN THE FACE OF JESUS CHRIST. 2 CORINTHIANS 4:6
While it may seem like all is dark, for those who trust in the Lord, His light is within us guiding us even on the darkest days. Take time to experience His light working from within.

NOW FROM THE SIXTH HOUR THERE WAS DARKNESS OVER ALL THE LAND UNTO THE NINTH HOUR. MATTHEW 27:45
AND, BEHOLD, THERE WAS A GREAT EARTHQUAKE: FOR THE ANGEL OF THE LORD DESCENDED FROM HEAVEN, AND CAME AND ROLLED BACK THE STONE FROM THE DOOR, AND SAT UPON IT. HIS COUNTENANCE WAS LIKE LIGHTNING, AND HIS RAIMENT WHITE AS SNOW: AND FOR FEAR OF HIM THE KEEPERS DID SHAKE, AND BECAME AS DEAD MEN. AND THE ANGEL ANSWERED AND SAID UNTO THE WOMEN, FEAR NOT YE: FOR I KNOW THAT YE SEEK JESUS, WHICH WAS CRUCIFIED. HE IS NOT HERE:

FOR HE IS RISEN, AS HE SAID. COME, SEE THE PLACE WHERE THE LORD LAY. MATTHEW 28:2-6

As Christ hung on the cross, darkness filled the land. I am sure the disciples and all who were there that day felt that darkness. We may have times that we feel like we are in our darkest moment but just like the disciples discovered there will always come a new light. Give it all to Jesus today.

WHILE THE EARTH REMAINETH, SEEDTIME AND HARVEST, AND COLD AND HEAT, AND SUMMER AND WINTER, AND DAY AND NIGHT SHALL NOT CEASE. GENESIS 8:22

God has promised that as long as the earth is here, we will have a change in seasons. So, if this winter has been long, trust that God is bringing the Spring! Rejoice in His promises.

Spring

There is nothing quite like a nice Spring day! The chill of winter is starting to fade and the buds begin to peak through on what appeared to be lifeless trees. The warm breeze is a refreshing delight from the cold winds of winter. As you venture out into the world you will notice the signs of new life emerging all around which can put a little giddy up in your step.

We experience spring in our lives as well. The news of a pregnancy, a new career, a wedding, or even a new friend can bring an excitement into the everyday routine of life. We begin to make plans for the future with excitement of all the possibilities.

If it is a pregnancy we begin to nest, putting together a list of names, buying baby clothes, decorating the nursery for the joyful upcoming day. With a new job, we orient ourselves with the ins and outs of the company, learn our job responsibilities and meet new coworkers. If it is a wedding, we start planning for the cake, the location, food, dress and all the little details of creating the perfect big day.

Spring will also make itself known in our walk with Christ. When we first feel the Spirit knock on our heart's door, we can sense newness but when we surrender our lives to Christ as Lord and Saviour... everything becomes new. We now have a new life everything has potential! The way we look at ourselves and at others becomes new. We now have a new-found hope in this life, a hope that reminds us that we will never walk alone, that we do not have to fear what life brings our way because the very one that gave us life is guiding us.

This newness is not just when we accept Christ as Lord and Saviour, but we will experience it throughout our faith walk. God will lead us to new adventures in home ministry or missions. We will be sitting in our quiet time reading a very familiar passage but, this time, the Holy Spirit reveals it to you in a whole new light, a way that brings renewed hope and/or excitement for the word and this journey He has put you on. This is the refreshing part of Spring; it isn't just for a moment. It is a season that comes back around when you least expect it.

Spring also tends to bring the rain. Showers to water the earth, to encourage the new buds to blossom. Showers are not always our favorite part of the season but are a necessity if we want the beauty of the flowers and the trees. We must have water to refresh nature to its newfound glory each year.

There is an old hymn, Showers of Blessings wrote by Daniel Webster Whittle that says:

> *Showers of blessing,*
> *Showers of blessing we need;*
> *Mercy-drops round us are falling,*
> *But for the showers we plead.*

When it rains this hymn comes to my mind. How marvelous it is that God not only sends rain to water the earth so nature can grow and develop into new life, but He also sends showers to water our souls with the refreshing blessings of heaven. The Bible teaches us that His mercies are new every morning if we will just seek them.

After the long enduring days of winter, spring can become an overflowing of encouragement and hope. I'm sure that the cross seemed like the coldest and darkest day of winter for all that followed Jesus, but little did they know that in three days, Spring was coming!! Christ would defeat hell, death and the grave and rise victorious for all to have a way to new life, making spring available every day of the year for all who would believe.

As I was working on this devotion, I was so excited as the Lord kept reminding me of the ultimate spring at His resurrection. I had to just stop and shout but in that I felt the Spirit remind me that for me that isn't the best spring to come because for the child of God, Jesus rose up out of that grave and our best Spring is yet to come.

Stick with me, we might face many seasons here on earth, we might have many ups and downs. There may come a time when the winter is overwhelming and we don't see a ray of sunlight but oh, son or daughter of the King, that is when you need to let the sweet breeze of heaven blow across your soul and remind you that SPRING IS COMING!

When this life is over and the devil thinks winter has won, we will open our eyes in the presence of the One who died for us, and our forever Spring will begin.

FOR, LO, THE WINTER IS PAST, THE RAIN IS OVER [AND] GONE; THE FLOWERS APPEAR ON THE EARTH; THE TIME OF THE SINGING [OF BIRDS] IS COME, AND THE VOICE OF THE TURTLE IS HEARD IN OUR LAND; THE FIG TREE PUTTETH FORTH HER GREEN FIGS, AND THE VINES [WITH] THE TENDER GRAPE GIVE A [GOOD] SMELL. ARISE, MY LOVE, MY FAIR ONE, AND COME AWAY. SONG OF SOLOMON 2:11-13

Is there a new thing springing up from within you? Do you feel like the Lord is leading you to a new beginning? Spend some time writing it out. If you are currently in a different season of life, ask the Lord to start preparing you for the spring to come.

Take a moment and write out Isaiah 43:19 and read it out loud several times throughout your day.

IT IS OF THE LORD'S MERCIES THAT WE ARE NOT CONSUMED, BECAUSE HIS COMPASSIONS FAIL NOT. THEY ARE NEW EVERY MORNING: GREAT IS THY FAITHFULNESS. THE LORD IS MY PORTION, SAITH MY SOUL; THEREFORE WILL I HOPE IN HIM. LAMENTATIONS 3:22-24

Put this verse where you will be able to see it multiple times each day. Remind yourself that the Lord has new mercies for you every morning.

FOR AS THE EARTH BRINGETH FORTH HER BUD, AND AS THE GARDEN CAUSETH THE THINGS THAT ARE SOWN IN IT TO SPRING FORTH; SO THE LORD GOD WILL CAUSE RIGHTEOUSNESS AND PRAISE TO SPRING FORTH BEFORE ALL THE NATIONS. ISAIAH 61:11

Maybe you are currently in a cold and long winter. You may be longing for the sun to shine hot and bright. Don't stop trusting and hoping in the Lord because it is He that will bring the spring at the right moment. A moment that will bring Him the most glory from your life. Write out a prayer of renewed trust, that God's timing is worth waiting on.

ABOUT THE AUTHOR

Mitzi is just an ordinary woman in love with an Almighty God. She currently resides in Dallas, North Carolina with her amazing husband, Rick Ivey. Mitzi is the president and founder of Finding the More Ministries, which is a nonprofit organization helping women discover More in their relationship with Jesus through outreach, bible study and weekly encouragement at Findingthemore.org.